Mother Nature's Pedagogy

Mother Nature's Pedagogy

Biological Foundations for
Children's Self-Directed Education

PETER GRAY

TIPPING POINTS PRESS
The Alliance for Self-Directed Education
CAMBRIDGE, MA, USA

Published by Tipping Points Press
The Alliance for Self-Directed Education

First paperback edition published in 2020 by Tipping Points Press

ISBN: 978-1-952837-06-7 (paperback)
ISBN: 978-1-952837-07-4 (ebook)

Library of Congress Cataloging-in-Publication Data
Names: Gray, Peter, author.
Title: Mother Nature's Pedagogy: Biological Foundations for Children's Self-
    Directed Education
Description: Tipping Points Press, The Alliance for Self-Directed Education
    [2020] | Includes biographical references and index.
Subjects: Alternative education, Child Development, Evolutionary psychology.
Identifiers: ISBN 978-1-952837-06-7 (paperback) | ISBN 978-1-952837-07-4
    (ebook)

The chapters published in this book were previously published as separate articles in Peter Gray's column, "Freedom to Learn" in *Psychology Today* and are presented here with permission.

Cover Illustration Credit: Paikea Melcher

Cover & Interior Design Credit: Elliott Beard

Contents

Editor's Preface

Myriad thinkers before our time have diagnosed the ills of conventional educational systems and prescribed their cures. Dr. Peter Gray's magnificent contributions to this vital field, however, transcend the familiar routine of pointing out problems and proposing new methods to replace them. He rightly reframes the issue in the broader terms of civil liberties—in particular, the rights of children—and identifies the primary need for young people to take back their childhood. Peter has spent a remarkable 36-year career researching the relationship children have historically had with play and learning in their societies since the time of hunters and gatherers. In doing so, he has established a broad, humanitarian view of childhood that counteracts our culture's myopic, impersonal focus on assessment and workforce training. This compendium of essays, categorized by subject, catalogues the complete thoughts thus far of Dr. Gray's research on the importance of childhood freedom.

Peter's research and writing have made significant impacts on diverse populations concerned with the wellbeing and education of children, shifting his readers' thinking on children's rights and their understanding of what childhood has looked like over the history of humankind. I have heard innumerable firsthand accounts of the effect of Peter's work on parents, educators, play advocates, young people, and youth rights activists ranging from Sub-Saharan Africa to the Baltic States and from East Asia to South America. For example, a mother in Greece told me how Peter's writing motivated her to withdraw her child from the local school system and start a democratic education movement. A Sudbury school struggling to open in Turkey, where Self-Directed Education is illegal, attested to me that his writing inspired them to try it despite the risk and difficulty. A teenager in the U.S. Midwest attributed Peter's writing as the foundation of her effort to drop out of school and become an unschooler.

This begs the question, what is it about Dr. Gray's insightful research and writing that universally seems to inspire a new generation to risk breaking with convention and to actualize freedom through education, parenting, and personal growth? I cannot speak for all, but I think I may have an inkling. Peter's experience as a research professor of evolutionary, developmental, and educational psychology gives him an advantageous perspective on the subject of child rearing and learning. He is able to draw his readers out of society's normative obsession with assessment and workforce productivity, and compel us to pursue the deeper question of "What is it all for?" He backs up his perspectives with primary research, valid scientific evidence, and detailed explanations of the long history of self-directed childhoods.

In his 2013 book, *Free to Learn: Why Unleashing the Instinct to Play Will Make Our Children Happier, More Self-Reliant, and Better Students for Life*, Dr. Gray grounds his views in rigorous evolutionary research on the universal ways in which indigenous hunters and gatherers raised their young. His analysis shows that children are healthiest and learn most effectively when they are left to playfully explore their natural curiosities in a nurturing environment equipped with the tools of their culture. Dr. Gray observes that for hundreds of thousands of years, constituting nearly all of human history, this was the way in which children were raised. In other words, our species has survived throughout nearly all of our history by being trustful parents, and allowing children to self direct their own childhoods. This realization has given me, and many others, the knowledge and courage to depart and divest from the unnatural, unhealthy, and unjust attitude toward childhood that prevails in most cultures today.

Peter Gray's dedication and contribution to the subject of children's rights has inspired a new generation of advocates, now equipped with his scientific evidence of what is the long-established, just, and healthy way for children to thrive in their development. This compendium of essays, assembled and adapted from his column "Freedom to Learn," appearing in *Psychology Today*, presents the many years of findings and reporting of Dr. Gray's lifelong work. It is a contemporary reader's great fortune to have this compilation available for inspiration and documentation. And it is my great honor to provide you with this work, which also initiates a hopefully long tradition of forthcoming books about the rights of the child. This compendium marks the inaugural publication of Tipping Points Press, dedicated to the advocacy of children's rights, by the Alliance for Self-Directed Education, which Peter Gray helped to found. We look forward to the continuation of pushing forward in advocating for children's rights until we reach that tipping point, when all children are free.

> *Alexander Khost*
> Editor-in-Chief
> Tipping Points Press
> The Alliance for Self-Directed Education
> APRIL 18, 2020

Author's Preface

I have been writing a blog for *Psychology Today* magazine, called "Freedom to Learn," since July, 2008. I have been posting there, at a rate of roughly one per month, articles dealing with child development and education, especially with children's natural ways of educating themselves when they are free to do so.

Over the years I have received many requests, from readers, for bound collections of these articles, arranged by topic, which would make the articles easier to find and easier to give to others than is possible by searching the *Psychology Today* online contents. Now, in collaboration with Tipping Points Press, the new book-publishing arm of the Alliance for Self-Directed Education (ASDE), I am responding to that request.

We are beginning with four collections, published simultaneously. The collection you have in hand is about the natural, biological drives that underlie children's self-education and the conditions that optimize those drives. The other collections in this set deal, respectively, with the harm to children that is perpetrated by our system of compulsory schooling; the evidence that Self-Directed Education works (that children in charge of their own education educate themselves well); and how children acquire academic skills (especially literacy and numeracy) when allowed to do so in their own ways. The essays have in some cases been modified slightly from the original *Psychology Today* versions, for clarity and to add more recent information.

I thank Rachel Wallach for her excellent, volunteer work in copyediting this collection; Paikea Melcher, who is a young person engaged in Self-Directed Education, for creating the cover illustration; and Alexander Khost, Editor-in-Chief of Tipping Point Press, for making these collections possible. I also thank the editors of *Psychology Today* for their support over the years in my posting these articles.

All profits from the sales of this book and others in the set help support ASDE in its mission to make opportunities for Self-Directed Education available to all families that seek it.

Peter Gray

1

Biological Foundations for Self-Directed Education

Four powerful, innate drives that lead children to educate themselves

SEPTEMBER 28, 2016

Children come into the world biologically designed to educate themselves. Some of the evidence for this, which I have described elsewhere (in Collection 2 in this series, and Gray, 2016, 2017), comes from observing the amazing learning capacities of children before they start school, the ways that children and adolescents in hunter-gatherer cultures educate themselves, and the ways that children today educate themselves at democratic schools and in unschooling families.

The biological design for self-directed education lies largely in four powerful natural drives: curiosity, playfulness, sociability and planfulness. The foundations for these drives are encoded in our DNA, shaped by natural selection over our evolutionary history to serve the purpose of education.

Schools quite deliberately suppress these drives, especially the first three, in the interest of promoting conformity and keeping children focused on the school's curriculum. In contrast, self-directed education—as it occurs in unschooling families and at democratic schools—operates by allowing these natural drives to flourish. Here I will elaborate on each of these drives and how they interact with one another to promote education.

1. Curiosity

Aristotle began his great treatise on the origin of knowledge, *Metaphysica*, with the words, "Human beings are naturally curious about things." Nothing could be truer. We are intensely curious from the moment of our birth to, in many cases, the moment of our death. Within hours of birth, infants begin to look at novel objects for longer periods than at those they have already seen. As they gain mobility, first with their arms and hands and then with their legs, they use that mobility to explore ever-larger realms of their environment. They want to understand the objects in their environment, and they particularly want to know what they can do with those objects. That is why they are continuously getting into things, always exploring. Once they have language, their curiosity drives them to ask many questions. Such curiosity does not diminish as children grow older, unless schooling quashes it, but continues to motivate ever more sophisticated modes of exploration and experimentation over ever larger spans of their environment. Children are, by nature, scientists.

2. Playfulness

The drive to play serves educative purposes complementary to those of curiosity. While curiosity motivates children to seek new knowledge and understanding, playfulness motivates them to practice new skills and use those skills creatively. Children everywhere, when they are free to do so and have plenty of playmates, spend enormous amounts of time playing. They play to have fun, not deliberately to educate themselves, but education is the side effect for which the strong drive to play evolved. Children play in order to develop the full range of skills that are crucial to their long-term survival and well-being:

- They play in physical ways as they climb, chase, and rough-and-tumble, and that is how children develop strong bodies and graceful movement.

- They play in risky ways, and that is how they learn to manage fear and develop courage.

- They play with language, and that is how they become competent with language.

- They play games with implicit or explicit rules, and that is how they learn to follow rules.

- They play imaginative games, and that is how they learn to think hypothetically and creatively.

- They play with logic, and that is how they become logical.

- They play at building things, and that is how they learn to build.

- They play with the tools of their culture, and that is how they become skilled at using those tools.

- And, most important of all, when they are free to do so, they play socially, with other children, and that is how they learn to negotiate, compromise, and get along with peers.

Play is not recess from education; it IS education. Children learn far more in play, and with far more joy, than they could possibly learn in a classroom.

3. Sociability

We humans are not only the most curious and playful of mammals, but also among the most social. Our children come into the world with an instinctive understanding that their survival and well-being depend on their ability to connect with and learn from other people. All humans, but especially young ones, want to know what those around them know and share their own thoughts and knowledge with others. Anthropologists report that children everywhere learn more by watching and listening to the people around them than through any other means (Lancy et al, 2010).

Our most unique adaptation for social life, which tremendously enhances our ability to learn from one another, is language. Almost as soon as they can talk, children start to ask questions. They don't want to be told about things that don't interest them, but they almost demand to be told about things that do. Language allows us to share all sorts of information with one another. It allows us to tell one another not just about the here and now, but also about the past, future, and hypothetical. As the philosopher Daniel Dennett (1994) wrote in a chapter on language and intelligence, "Comparing our brains with bird brains or dolphin brains is almost beside the point, because our brains are in effect joined together into a single cognitive system that dwarfs all others. They are joined by an innovation that has invaded our brain and no others: language." Self-directed learners, eagerly and naturally, hook themselves into that network. Today, because of the Internet, that cognitive system is bigger than ever before. Young people with access to the Internet have access to the whole world of hypotheses, ideas, and information. Self-directed education has never been easier.

4. Planfulness

Humans, far more than any other species, have the capacity to think ahead. In fact, we are driven to do so. We don't just react to immediate situations; we anticipate future situations, make plans for them, and follow through on those plans. This is the most consciously cognitive of our basic educative drives, and it develops more slowly than the others. As children grow older, they become increasingly able and motivated to plan ahead, and ever further ahead. This is the drive that leads self-directed learners to think about their life goals, big and small, and to deliberately seek out the knowledge and practice the skills needed to achieve those goals. Cognitive scientists refer to this capacity to make plans and carry them out as self-directed executive functioning. Research by such scientists has shown that children who have ample free time to play and explore on their own and with other children, independent of adults, develop this capacity more fully than children who spend more time in adult-structured activities (Barker et al, 2014). That is not surprising. When children create their own activities, without adult control, they continuously practice the ability to make plans and carry them out. They make mistakes, but they learn from those mistakes.

So, we don't have to educate children. Indeed, our attempts to do so inhibit children's education because they interfere with their natural ways of learning through exploring, playing, paying attention to and communicating with others, and planning their own activities. Our job concerning our children's education is to make sure that they have full range to use their natural educative instincts, and get out of their way except for when they want our help.

References

Barker, J. et al (2014). Less-structured time in children's lives predicts self-directed executive functioning. *Frontiers in Psychology*, 5, 1-16.

Dennett, D. C. (1994). Language and intelligence. In J. Khalfa (Ed.), *What is intelligence?* Cambridge: Cambridge University Press.

Gray, P. (2016). Children's natural ways of learning still work—even for the three Rs. In D. C. Geary & D. B. Berch (eds), *Evolutionary perspectives on child development and education* (pp 63-93). Springer.

Gray, P. (2017). Self-directed education—unschooling and democratic schooling. In G. Noblit (Ed.), *Oxford research encyclopedia of education*. New York: Oxford University Press.

Lancy, D. F., Bock, J., & Gaskins, S. (2010). Putting learning into context. In D. F. Lancy, J. Bock, & S. Gaskins (Eds.) *The anthropology of learning in childhood*, 3–10. Lanham, MD: AltaMira Press.

2

Minimally Invasive Education

Lessons from India

*How thousands of impoverished children
in India became computer literate*

JANUARY 28, 2009

On January 29, 1999, Sugata Mitra—who, at the time, was science director of an information technology firm in New Delhi—initiated a fascinating set of studies of children's self-directed learning. On that day, he installed a computer in an outside wall of the firm's building, a wall that faced one of the poorest slums in New Delhi, a community where most children at that time did not go to school, were illiterate, and had never previously seen a computer. He simply turned the computer on, left it there, told the crowd of children that they could play with it, and used a video camera to monitor activity around it.

Children—mostly in the age range of 6 to 13—immediately approached and began to explore this odd installment, which looked to them like some kind of television set. They touched some of the parts and, apparently by accident, discovered that they could move a pointer on the screen by moving their finger across the touch pad. This led to a series of further exciting discoveries. The pointer turned to a hand when it was moved to certain parts of the screen. By pushing (clicking) on the touch pad when the pointer was a hand, they could get the screen to change. They eagerly sought out their friends to tell them about this fascinating machine. Each new discovery, made by one child or a group, was shared with others. Within days, dozens of children were playing music and games, painting with Microsoft Paint, and doing many of the other things that children everywhere do with computers when they have access to them.

Subsequently, Mitra and his colleagues repeated the experiment in 26 other places in India, rural as well as urban, always with the same general results. Similar findings occurred in other nations where outdoor computers were set up—in Cambodia, Egypt, and South Africa.

Wherever a computer kiosk was set up, children quickly gathered, explored the apparatus, and, with no help except that which they provided to each other, discovered exciting ways to use it. The children made up names to refer to the computer, its parts, the various icons that appeared on the screen, and the activities they could perform with the computer. For example, one group referred (in their native Hindi language) to the pointer as a "needle" and to folders as "cupboards". Those who did not know English learned many English words through their interactions with the computer and through conversations with others about it. Children who could read sometimes found and downloaded articles that interested them, in the language in which they were literate (typically Hindi or Marathi).

Mitra and his colleagues describe the kind of education with which they were experimenting as minimally invasive education, a descriptor borrowed from the medical world of surgery. It is education with the minimal amount of intrusion into children's lives. The experiments demonstrated that children learned at an amazingly rapid rate with no adult teachers. All that the educators had to do was to provide the tool, in this case, the computer. The children's natural curiosity, playfulness, and sociability took over from there.

Mitra and his colleagues estimate that for each outdoor computer they set up, an average of 300 children became computer literate within three months of the computer's becoming available. That is 30,000 computer-literate children for 100 computers, within a three-month period. By computer literate, Mitra means that they could "do most or all of the following tasks":

- Use all Windows operational functions, such as click, drag, open, close, resize, minimize, open menus, navigate, etc.

- Draw and paint with the computer.

- Load and save files.

- Play games.

- Run educational and other programs.

▪ Browse and surf the Internet, if a connection is available.

▪ Set up email accounts.

▪ Send and receive email.

▪ Chat on the Internet.

▪ Do simple troubleshooting, for example, if the speakers are not working.

▪ Download and play streaming media.

▪ Download games.

On the basis of various tests given to randomly chosen children who used the outdoor computers, Mitra concluded that the children's abilities to learn in this setting "seem to be independent of their educational background, literacy levels in English or any other language, social or economic level, ethnicity and place of origin (city, town, or village), gender, genetic background, geographic location, and intelligence." (For references to this work, see Dangwal et al, 2006; Inamdar, 2004; Mitra, 2003, 2004, 2005; Mitra & Rana, 2001).

Mitra's observations beautifully illustrate many of the ideas that I have been discussing in my essays. My major theme is that children educate themselves. Mitra observed that children taught themselves to use the computer, and then used the computer to teach themselves much more. They did so because they have, within them, a set of powerful instincts for self-education—the instincts of curiosity, playfulness, and sociability.

Curiosity: All mammals are curious, but we humans are

the most curious, especially in childhood. Because we are tool-using animals, our curiosity leads us to explore new objects not just with our senses, but also with our muscles. When we see something new, we want to know what we can do with it. Children, from infancy on, explore new objects by manipulating them—pushing them, shaking them, squeezing them, dropping them, throwing them, bouncing them—to see what interesting effects might be produced. In Mitra's experiments, curiosity drew children to the outdoor computer and motivated them to manipulate it in various ways to learn about its properties. The manipulations led to exciting discoveries, each of which led to new questions and new discoveries. For example, the discovery that clicking on one icon caused the screen to change led children to click on all of the other available icons, just to see what would happen.

Playfulness: The young of nearly all mammals are playful, but young humans are the most playful of all. The primary evolutionary function of playfulness, in children and other young mammals, is skill development (Gray, 2019). Play involves repetitive actions, with some variation from trial to trial, aimed at producing effects that the player has in mind. The actions—both physical and mental—are performed for the pure pleasure of doing them, but the consequence is skill in performing those actions. In Mitra's experiments, playfulness led children to become highly skilled at using the computer's functions. For example, children who had already explored the Paint program and knew how to use it were motivated to play with that program, that is, to use it to paint many pictures. Through such play those children became skilled at computer painting. Through play the children consolidated knowledge already acquired and developed skill in using that knowledge. Often play led inadvertently to new discoveries, which renewed curiosity and led to new bouts of exploration. Play and exploration are inseparably entwined.

Sociability: We humans are not only the supremely curious and playful animal, but also a supremely social animal. Our sociability is such that we want to know what other people know and to share what we know with others. This, perhaps more than anything else, is what distinguishes us from the other mammals. Through language and our desire to communicate with and understand others, our minds are linked in a vast network with the minds of other people. No other animal has such a capacity and drive for communication, and that is why no other animal has developed culture as we have. In Mitra's experiments, sociability motivated the children to play together, gave them the desire to know and do what the others knew and were doing, and drove them to share their own knowledge with others. When one child made a new discovery about something that could be done with the computer, that discovery spread like a brush fire through the whole group of children nearby; and then some child in that group, who had a friend in another group, would carry the spark of new knowledge to that other group, where a new brush fire was ignited, and so on, through the roughly 300 children who at varying times were using the computer. Each discovery by one child became the discovery of everyone in the network.

Why don't school lessons spread in the same wildfire way

that Mitra observed in his experiments on minimally invasive education? It is not hard to think of many answers to this question. Here are a few that come to mind:

- Children in school are not free to pursue their own, self-chosen interests, and this mutes their enthusiasm.

- Children in school are constantly evaluated. The concern for evaluation and pleasing the teacher—or, for some children, a rebellious reaction against such evaluation—overrides and subverts the possibility of developing genuine interest in the assigned tasks.

- Children in school are often shown one and only one way to solve a problem and are told that other ways are incorrect, so the excitement of discovering new ways is quashed.

- Segregation of children by age in schools prevents the age mixing and diversity that seem to be key to children's natural ways of learning. Mitra observed that the mix of abilities and interests in the age-mixed groups that gathered around the outdoor computers ensured that different functions of the computer were tried out and played with by different children and that a wide variety of discoveries were made, which could then spread from child to child.

Learning is joyful and exciting, when it occurs naturally. We make learning hard and dreary in our classrooms by depriving children of the opportunity to use their natural ways of learning and by replacing them with coercion. If we would concentrate on providing children with environments and tools that optimize their abilities to teach themselves, in age-mixed groups, and if we would stop trying to control children's learning, life would be more fun for all of us and the culture would flourish even more than it does now.

References

Dangwal, R., Jha, S., & Kapur, P. (2006). Impact of minimally invasive education on children: An Indian perspective. *British Journal of Educational Technology, 37*, 295-298.

Gray, P. (2019). Evolutionary functions of play: Practice, resilience, innovation, and cooperation. In P. K. Smith & J. Roopnarine (Eds.), *The Cambridge handbook of play: developmental and disciplinary perspectives* (pp 84-102). Cambridge, UK: Cambridge University Press.

Inamdar, P. (2004). Computer skills development by children using 'hole in the wall' facilities in rural India. *Australasian Journal of Educational Technology, 20*, 337-350.

Mitra, S. (2003). Minimally invasive education: A progress report on the "hole-in-the-wall" experiments. *British Journal of Educational Technology, 34*, 267-371.

Mitra, S. (2004). Hole in the wall. Dataquest (India), Sept. 23 issue.

Mitra, S. (2005). Self organizing systems for mass computer literacy: Findings from the "hole in the wall" experiments. *International Journal of Development Issues, 4*, 71-81.

Mitra, S., & Rana, V. (2001). Children and the internet: Experiments with minimally invasive education in India. *British Journal of Educational Technology, 32*, 221-232.

3

The Natural Environment for Children's Self-Education

*How the Sudbury Valley School is
like a hunter-gatherer band*

SEPTEMBER 3, 2008

A major theme of this volume is that we come into the world with instincts that are well designed to promote our education. We have instincts to observe, explore, play, and converse with others in ways that endow us with the skills, knowledge, and values needed to live and thrive in the physical and social world into which we are born. We do this with great intensity and joy. These educational instincts were shaped by natural selection during the hundreds of thousands of years in which our ancestors survived as hunter-gatherers (e.g., Gray, 2012). We might expect, therefore, that these instincts would operate best in the social environment of a hunter-gatherer band, or in a modern environment that replicates certain aspects of a hunter-gatherer band.

Ever since its founding in 1968, the Sudbury Valley School has been proving that the human instincts for self-education can provide the foundation for education in our modern society. At this school, children and adolescents explore, play, and converse as they please—without adult direction or prodding—and then graduate and go out into the world as successful adults (Gray, 2017). I have spent a good deal of time observing Sudbury Valley to understand how students learn there, and I have also surveyed the anthropological literature to understand how hunter-gatherer children and adolescents learn. This research has convinced me that Sudbury Valley works so well as an educational institution because it replicates those elements of a hunter-gatherer band that are most essential to self-directed education (Gray, 2016).

Here I offer a list of what seem to be the most crucial ingredients of the natural environment for self-directed learning. Anthropologists report that these ingredients exist in the hunter-gather bands they have studied (e.g., Hewlett et al, 2011; Hewlett & Lamb, 2005), and I have seen that all of them exist also at the Sudbury Valley School.

Time and Space for Play and Exploration

Self-education through play and exploration requires enormous amounts of unscheduled time—time to do whatever one wants to do, without pressure, judgment, or intrusion from authority figures. That time is needed to make friends, play with ideas and materials, experience and overcome boredom, solve problems, and develop passionate interests. In hunter-gatherer bands adults place few demands on children and adolescents, because they recognize that young people need to explore and play on their own in order to become competent adults. The same is true at Sudbury Valley.

Self-education also requires space—space to roam, to get away, to explore. That space should, ideally, encompass the full range of terrains relevant to the culture in which one is developing. Hunter-gatherer adults trust their children to use good judgment in deciding how far they should venture away from others into possibly dangerous areas. At Sudbury Valley, children are likewise trusted, within the limits set by prudence in our modern, litigious society. They can explore the surrounding woods, fields, and nearby stream, and by signing out to let others know where they are going, they can venture as far off campus as they choose.

Free Age Mixing

An enormous amount of learning occurs in interactions with others. When we segregate children by age, as we do in schools, we deprive them of the opportunity to interact with those others from whom they have the most to learn. In hunter-gatherer bands, and at Sudbury Valley, children and adolescents regularly, on their own initiative, play and explore in widely age-mixed groups.

In age-mixed groups, younger children acquire skills, information, ideas, and inspiration from older ones. In such groups, younger children can do things that would be too dangerous, or too complicated, for them to do alone or just with others their own age. Older children also benefit from age-mixed interactions. They learn how to be leaders and nurturers. They develop a sense of responsibility for others. They also consolidate and extend their own knowledge through explaining things to younger children. Free age mixing is so crucial to self-directed education that I will devote the next three essays of this collection to this topic.

Access to Knowledgeable and Caring Adults

In hunter-gatherer bands, the adult world is not segregated from the children's world. Children observe what adults do and incorporate those activities into their play. They also hear the adults' stories, discussions, and debates, and they learn from what they hear. When they need adult help or have questions that cannot be answered by other children, they can go to any of the adults in the band (Hewlett et al, 2011). All of the adults care for them. Most of the adults, in fact, are their aunts and uncles.

At Sudbury Valley, too, adults and children mingle freely (at the time of this writing there are about eight full-time staff members and 180 students, between the ages of 4 and 19). There is no place in the school where staff members can go but students cannot. Students can listen in to any adult discussions, observe whatever the adults are doing, and join in if they wish. Students who need help of any kind can go to any of the staff members. A child who needs a lap to sit on, or a shoulder to cry on, or personal advice, or the answer to some technical question that he hasn't been able to find on his own, knows just which adult will best satisfy his need. The adults are not literally aunts and uncles, but they are much like aunts and uncles. They know all of the students over the entire span of time that they are students at the school (unlike teachers in a conventional school) and take pride in watching them develop. Since the staff members must be re-elected each year by vote of all of the students in the school, they are necessarily people who like children and are liked by the children at the school.

Access to Equipment

In order to learn to use the tools of a culture, people need access to those tools. Hunter-gatherer children play with knives, digging sticks, bows and arrows, snares, musical instruments, dugout canoes, and all of the other items of equipment that are crucial to their particular culture. At Sudbury Valley, children have access to a wide range of the kind of equipment that is of use to people in our culture, including computers, woodworking equipment, cooking equipment, art materials, sporting equipment of various types, and a great variety of books.

Free Exchange of Ideas

Intellectual development occurs best in a setting where people can share ideas freely, without censorship or fear of being ostracized. According to reports by anthropologists, hunter-gatherers are non-dogmatic in their beliefs, even in their religious beliefs. People can say what they please without fear, and ideas that have any consequence to the group are debated endlessly. The same is true at Sudbury Valley. The school has deliberately refrained from becoming aligned with any particular religious or political ideology. All ideas are on the table. In this kind of environment an idea is something to think about and debate, not something to memorize and regurgitate on a test. Daniel Greenberg, the school's leading philosopher, has described the school as "a free marketplace of ideas". Children who may not hear much discussion of politics or religion at home hear it at school, and they are likely to hear every side of every issue.

Freedom from Bullying

To feel free to explore and play a person must feel safe, free from harassment and bullying. Such freedom occurs to a remarkable extent both in hunter-gatherer bands and at Sudbury Valley. According to anthropologists, the close-knit personal relationships, the age mixing, and the non-competitive, egalitarian ethos of hunter-gatherer cultures work effectively to prevent serious bullying. If an older or bigger child appears to be picking on a younger or smaller one, others will step in and quickly stop it. The same occurs at Sudbury Valley. Moreover, at Sudbury Valley the school's democratically created rules and judicial system, in which children of all ages are involved, prevent serious bullying. Students who feel harassed or bullied can "bring up" the offender, to appear before the Judicial Committee, which is comprised of school members of all ages. This contrasts sharply with the case in many conventional schools, where bullying is a way of life. Students who report bullying in conventional schools are regarded by their peers as snitches or tattletales, and teachers can get away with bullying because they make the rules and are not subject to them.

Immersion in Democratic Processes

Hunter-gatherer bands and the Sudbury Valley School are, in quite different ways, democracies. Hunter-gatherers do not have chiefs or "big men" who make decisions for the group (Lee, 1988). Instead, all group decisions are made through long discussions, until a clear majority of those who care have come to agreement. Children may not take much part in these discussions, but they hear them and grow up knowing that they will take part as they get older. Sudbury Valley is administered through a formal democratic process, involving discussions and votes of the School Meeting, where each student and staff member who chooses to attend has an equal vote. Immersion in the democratic process endows each person with a sense of responsibility that helps to motivate education. If my voice counts, if I have a real say in what the group does and how it operates, then I'd better think things through carefully and speak wisely. I'm responsible not just for myself, but also for my community, so that is a good reason for me to educate myself in the things that matter to my community.

In sum, my contention is that a natural environment for learning—which existed during our long history as hunter-gatherers and is replicated at the Sudbury Valley School—is one in which people (a) have plenty of free time and space in which to play and explore; (b) can mix freely with others of all ages; (c) have access to culturally relevant tools and equipment and are free to play and explore with those items; (d) are free to express and debate any ideas that they wish to express and debate; (e) are free from bullying (which includes freedom from being ordered around arbitrarily by adults); and (f) have a voice that is heard in the group's decision-making process.

How different this is from the environment of conventional schools. How ironic: In conventional schools we deprive children of all of the elements of a natural environment for education, and then we try to educate them.

References

Gray, P. (2012). The value of a play-filled childhood in development of the hunter-gatherer individual. In Narvaez, D., Panksepp, J., Schore, A., & Gleason, T. (Eds.), *Evolution, early experience and human development: from research to practice and policy*, pp 252-370. New York: Oxford University Press.

Gray, P. (2016). Children's natural ways of learning still work— even for the three Rs. In D. C. Geary & D. B. Berch (Eds.), *Evolutionary perspectives on child development and education,* pp 63-93. Springer.

Gray, P. (2017). Self-directed education—unschooling and democratic schooling. In G. Noblit (Ed.), *Oxford research encyclopedia of education*. New York: Oxford University Press.

Hewlett, B., Fouts, H., Boyette, A., & Hewlett, B. L. (2011). Social learning among Congo Basin hunter-gatherers. *Philosophical Transactions of the Royal Society B*, 366, 1168–1178.

Hewlett, B. & Lamb, M. (Eds.) (2005). *Hunter-gatherer childhoods: Evolutionary, developmental, and cultural perspectives.* Transaction Publishers.

Lee, R. B. (1988). Reflections on primitive communism. In T. Ingold, D. Riches & J. Woodburn (Eds.), *Hunters and gatherers 1.* Oxford: Berg

4

Why We Should Stop Segregating Children by Age

Part I

Children learn by playing in the zone of proximal development

SEPTEMBER 9, 2008

One of the oddest, and in my view most harmful, aspects our treatment of children today is our penchant for segregating them into separate groups by age. We do that not only in schools, but in out-of-school settings as well. In doing so, we deprive children of a valuable component of their natural means of self-education.

The age-segregated mode of schooling became dominant at about the same time in history that the assembly-line approach to manufacturing became dominant. The implicit analogy is clear. The graded school system treats children as if they are items on an assembly line, moving from stop to stop (grade to grade) along a conveyor belt, all at the same speed. At each stop a factory worker (teacher) adds some new component (unit of knowledge) to the product. At the end of the line, the factory spits out complete, new, adult human beings, all built to the specifications of the manufacturers (the professional educators).

Of course, everyone who has ever known a child, including everyone who works in our age-graded schools, knows that this assembly-line view of child development is completely false. Children are not passive products, to which we can add components. Children are not incomplete adults that need to be built bit by bit in some ordered sequence. Children are complete human being, who constantly demand to control their own lives and who, despite what we put them through, insist on learning what they want to learn and practicing the skills they want to practice. We would all be much better off if we went with them on this rather than fought them.

Elsewhere I have described settings where children educate themselves without adult direction or prodding. In particular, I have discussed self-education as it once occurred in hunter-gatherer bands and as it occurs today in schools designed for self-education, particularly the Sudbury Valley School (in Book 2 in this series and in Gray, 2016, 2017). A prominent feature of such settings is that children regularly interact with others across the whole spectrum of ages. Anthropologists have claimed that free age mixing is the key to the self-education of hunter-gatherer children; and Daniel Greenberg (1992) has long claimed that free age mixing is the key to self-education at the Sudbury Valley School, which he helped to found.

Some years ago, Jay Feldman (who then was a graduate student working with me) and I conducted some studies of age-mixed interactions at the Sudbury Valley School, aimed at determining how much age mixing occurred at the school and identifying ways by which age mixing seemed to contribute to students' education. The school has, at any given time, approximately 150 to 200 students, who range in age from 4 to 18 years old and sometimes older. Students can move freely at all times throughout the school buildings and campus, and they can interact with whomever they please. The school's population is large enough that students could, if they chose, interact just with others who are within a year or two of themselves in age. But they don't do that. In a study that involved multiple tours of the school over several days we found that more than 50% of students' social interactions at the school were with other students who were more than two years older or younger than themselves, and 25% were with other students who were more than 4 years older or younger than themselves (Gray & Feldman, 1997). Age mixing was especially frequent during play. Active play of all sorts was more likely to be age mixed than was conversation that did not involve play.

In a long-term qualitative study, in which we observed and made notes on approximately 200 interactions involving students who differed in age by at least four years, we identified many ways by which age mixing fosters the education of both the younger and older students involved (Gray & Feldman, 2004). Here I describe one of those ways, and in the next two essays I describe others.

In the 1930's, the Russian developmental psychologist Lev Vygotsky (English translation, 1978) developed a concept that he called the *zone of proximal development*, defined as the realm of activities that a child can accomplish in collaboration with more skilled others but cannot accomplish alone or with others who are at his or her same level. Vygotsky claimed that children learn best when they are engaged with more skilled others within their zones of proximal development. Since Vygotsky's time, education professors have often used this concept to describe interactions between adult teachers and young learners, but the concept applies far better, I think, to naturally occurring age-mixed interactions among children.

As an illustration, imagine two 4-year-olds trying to play a simple game of catch. They can't do it. Neither child can throw the ball straight enough for the other to catch it, so the game is no fun and quickly dissolves. Now imagine a 4-year-old playing catch with a skilled 8-year-old. The older child, by diving and leaping, can catch the wild throws of the younger one and can have fun doing so; and the older child can lob the ball directly into the outstretched hands of the younger one, so the latter can experience the joy of catching. Thus, catch is a game within the 4-year-old's zone of proximal development. In an age-segregated environment consisting of only 4-year-olds, there would be no possibility of playing catch; but in an age-mixed environment that includes some

8-year-olds as well as 4-year-olds, playing catch is within everyone's realm of possibility.

At any given time of day at Sudbury Valley one can find young children playing games with older children that they would not be able to play just with age-mates. These include intellectual games as well as athletic ones, and in nearly every case of such play we saw ways by which the older children boosted the younger ones up to a higher level of activity. For example, we observed 7- and 8-year-olds playing complicated card games with older children and teenagers. By themselves, the younger children would be unable to play such games. They would not be able to focus long enough, or keep track of the rules, or even remember to hold their cards straight enough to keep others from seeing them. They could, however, play the games with older children because the older ones kept them on track, reminded them when necessary of what they had to do, and sometimes gave them strategy hints: "Pay attention." "Try to remember which cards were played." "Think before you lay down a card, so you don't put down something another player can take." Attention, memory, and forethought are the elements of what we commonly call intelligence. In the process of playing cards, which they were only doing to have fun, the older children were incidentally helping the younger ones to develop their intelligence.

Vygotsky's concept also helps us understand how young children learn to read at Sudbury Valley. Children who can't read, or can't read well, can regularly be found playing games (especially computer games) that involve the written word with children who can read well. The readers read aloud what the others cannot, and in the process the non-readers gradually become readers themselves.

Age mixing also allows young children to engage in adventures that would be too dangerous for them to do alone or just with age mates. Children who would, quite appropriately, be too frightened to venture off into the woods by themselves feel safe doing so with older children, who know the woods. Similarly, little kids new to tree climbing feel safe venturing up onto some of the lower branches if big kids are under them, advising them how to do it, ready to catch them if they fall.

If you are little and can interact only with others your own age, the range of possible activities is restricted by the knowledge and abilities of those in your age group; but in collaboration with older children there is almost no limit to what you might do!

References

Gray, P. (2016). Children's natural ways of learning still work—even for the three Rs. In D. C. Geary & D. B. Berch (eds), *Evolutionary perspectives on child development and education* (pp 63-93). Springer.

Gray, P. (2017). Self-directed education—unschooling and democratic schooling. In G. Noblit (Ed.), *Oxford research encyclopedia of education*. New York: Oxford University Press.

Gray, P., & Feldman, J. (1997). Patterns of age mixing and gender mixing among children and adolescents at an ungraded democratic school. *Merrill-Palmer Quarterly*, 43, 67-86.

Gray, P., & Feldman, J. (2004). Playing in the zone of proximal development: qualities of self-directed age mixing between adolescents and young children at a democratic school. *American Journal of Education,* 110, 108-145.

Greenberg, D. (1992). Sudbury Valley's secret weapon: Allowing people of different ages to mix freely at school. In D. Greenberg (Ed.), *The Sudbury Valley School experience, 3rd ed.* Framingham, MA: Sudbury Valley School Press.

Vygotsky, L. (1978). Interaction between learning and development. In M. Cole, V. John-Steiner, S. Scribner, and E. Souberman (Eds), *Mind and society: the development of higher psychological processes.* Cambridge, MA: Harvard University Press.

5

Why We Should Stop Segregating Children by Age

Part II

Age-mixed play is more playful, less competitive, than same-age play

SEPTEMBER 17, 2008

During the long course of human history, play almost always occurred in age-mixed settings (Gray, 2011). The biological foundations for play evolved to serve educative purposes in settings where children were almost never segregated by age. Anthropologists who have studied play in hunter-gatherer groups report that a typical playgroup might range in age from age 4 through 12, or 8 through 17. When we observe play in age-segregated settings such as school playgrounds—where 6-year-olds can play only with other 6-year-olds and 12-year-olds only with other 12-year-olds—we are observing an artifact of modern times. Studying children's play in age-segregated settings is like studying monkeys in cages; we are observing behavior under unnaturally confined conditions. Monkeys in cages show a lot more aggression and dominance behavior than do monkeys in the wild, and the same is true of children in age-segregated settings compared to those in age-mixed settings.

In the first essay in this trilogy, I described how age-mixed play allows younger children to participate in, and learn from, activities that would be too difficult for them to do alone or just with age-mates. In this essay I will comment on some qualitative differences between age-mixed play and age-segregated play. My main point is this:

> *Age-mixed play is less competitive, more creative, and more conducive to practicing new skills than is same-age play.*

Age-mixed play is, in short, more playful than is same-age play. When children who are all nearly the same age play a game, competitiveness can interfere with playfulness. This is especially true in our current culture, which puts so much emphasis on winning and on all sorts of comparisons aimed at determining who is better, an emphasis fostered by our competitive, graded school system and by many other adult-directed activities into which children are placed. In contrast, when children who differ widely in age play a game together, the focus shifts from that of beating the other to that of having fun. There is no pride to be gained by the older, larger, more skilled child in beating the much younger one, and the younger one has no expectation of beating the older one. So, they play the game more joyfully, in a more relaxed manner, modifying the rules in ways that make it both fun and challenging for all involved. A playful mood facilitates creativity, experimentation, and the learning of new skills, while a competitive orientation tends to inhibit these and leads a person to fall back on skills that have already been well learned.

My own systematic studies of age-mixed play have taken place primarily at the Sudbury Valley School, where students age 4 through about 18 are free to interact with one another, as they please, at any time of day. In an essay that he wrote several years after graduating from Sudbury Valley, Michael Greenberg (1992) described age-mixed soccer games at the school. I offer the following rather extensive quotation from that essay, because it illustrates so beautifully some of the values of age-mixed play.

> One person says, "Let's play soccer" to some other people. Whoever feels like playing at the moment comes to the field. There are 6-year-olds, 10-year-olds, 18-year-olds, maybe a staff member or a parent who feels like joining in. There are boys and girls. Teams are chosen with a conscious effort at creating evenly matched sides. . . . [T]his often consists of one team having an extra "big kid" who can play well and the other team getting a small army of 6-year-olds to get in his way. People want even teams because they are playing for fun. It's no fun to play a game with lopsided teams. . . . The game is played by whoever wants to play, for as long as they feel like playing. There

will always be certain people who value winning, but there is little peer performance pressure. Most people don't really care who wins.

Now, you might get the impression that people are not trying very hard to be good at the game, but that's not true. The process of play is only fun if you exert effort and challenge yourself. That is why people developed the idea of games like soccer in the first place. Running around for no reason gets boring, but running around trying to kick a ball between two posts that are guarded by people who are trying to stop you—that's exciting.

The people who play sports as we do at [Sudbury Valley School] learn far more profound lessons about life than those that can be taught by regimented, performance-oriented sports. They learn teamwork—not the 'we against them' type of teamwork, but the teamwork of a diverse group of people of diverse talents organizing themselves to pursue a common activity—the teamwork of life. They learn excellence, not the 'I'm the star' type of excellence, but the type of excellence that comes from setting a standard for yourself to live up to and then trying your best to live up to it.

I'm 23 years old and I've played a lot of soccer. It would be pretty silly for me to try to be better than the three 8-year-olds who crowd around my feet every time I try to kick the ball. I think that the 8-year-olds are too busy running after kids who are three feet taller than they are to worry about being the best 8-year-old. In this game, as in real life, the only standard that matters is one you set for yourself. One of the profound truths you learn is that we are all so different from each other that peer pressure and comparisons of worth are meaningless. If you're 11 years old and you are only allowed to play with other 11-year-olds, it's very hard to glimpse this profound truth, which unlocks the meaning of excellence.

[They also] learn responsibility and restraint. In all the years of playing very physical games like football, soccer, and basketball, there has never been an injury beyond a minor cut or bruise. People play all these sports in their regular clothes without any of the standard protective equipment that is normally required. How can this be explained when people wearing protective pads injure each other with alarming frequency? Because in a regimented, performance-oriented way of looking at sports (or life), making sure you don't hurt someone becomes less important than winning. So it doesn't matter how much you talk about "sportsmanship" or how many safety pads you wear, people are going to get hurt. When you approach sports (or life) as a fun, exciting process, as something that is done for the sheer joy and beauty of doing it, then not hurting someone, not impairing their ability to enjoy the same process, becomes a top priority. . . .

To participate in an activity where the clash of unequal bodies is transformed through teamwork, pursuit of personal excellence, responsibility, and restraint into a common union of equal souls in pursuit of meaningful experience has been one of the most profound experiences of my life. I am sure it has had a similar effect on others.

In our systematic observations at Sudbury Valley, Jay Feldman and I recorded many occurrences of age-mixed play that fit well with Michael Greenberg's description (Gray & Feldman, 2004). In one instance, for example, Feldman watched a tall 15-year-old boy playing basketball with a group of much shorter 8- to 10-year-olds. The older boy rarely shot, but spent much time joyfully dribbling while the gang of small boys who made up the opposing team tried to steal the ball from him. Then he would pass to his single teammate (age 8) and encourage him to shoot. By dribbling and passing rather than shooting, the older boy made the game fun and challenging not just for the younger children but also for himself. Shooting baskets is too easy to be fun when nobody is tall enough to block your shots, but dribbling through a gang of short people who are trying to steal the ball is a great, fun way to improve your dribbling. Here's another example, quoted from one of our articles (Gray & Feldman, 2004), which illustrates the creative, light-hearted nature of age-mixed athletic play:

> In an age-mixed game of Capture the Flag, one team, the Big People, consisted of three adolescents and one 11-year-old, and the other team, the Hordes, consisted of ten 4- to 8-year-olds and one 12-year-old. Larry (age 4) would often run across the line and get captured by Sam (age 17) in an act that included lots of tickling and carrying of Larry in mock combat. After Larry was set down, he would prance merrily back to his side, without going to jail. Often one or more of the Big People would cross into the Hordes' territory not to go after the flag but simply to

run around with a gang of small children chasing them. Nobody seemed to be much focused on winning, but when the Hordes did finally capture the flag, they cheered loudly. [Note: Student names used here and throughout this essay and the next are pseudonyms.]

Board games and card games, likewise, are played in more playful, creative, non-competitive ways when the players vary widely in age than when they are age-mates. Feldman observed many games of chess, which happened to be a fad at the time of his research. Games between equally matched players tended to be quite serious; the players appeared intent on winning. Games between unmatched players, who usually differed widely in age, were more creative and light-hearted. To make the game interesting, the older players would typically self-handicap in some way, for example by deliberately getting into difficult positions, and would frequently point out better moves to the younger players. The older players seemed to be using such games to experiment with new styles of play, which they were not yet ready to try out in serious games.

Some of the most creative and joyful samples of play I have witnessed involved teenagers and younger children engaged together in shared fantasy play. Here is another quotation, describing one such scene that I observed (Gray, 2008):

I was sitting in the playroom at the Sudbury Valley School, ... pretending to read a book but surreptitiously observing a remarkable scene. A 13-year-old boy and two 7-year-old boys were creating, purely for their own amusement, a fantastic story involving heroic characters, monsters, and battles. The 7-year-olds gleefully shouted out ideas about what would happen next, while the 13-year-old, an excellent artist, translated the ideas into a coherent story and sketched the scenes on the blackboard almost as fast as the younger children could describe them. The game continued for at least half an hour, which was the length of time I permitted myself to watch before moving on. I felt privileged to enjoy an artistic creation that, I know, could not have been produced by 7-year-olds alone and almost certainly would not have been produced by 13-year-olds alone. The unbounded enthusiasm and creative imagery of the 7-year-olds I watched, combined with the advanced narrative and artistic abilities of the 13-year-old they played with, provided just the right chemical mix for this creative explosion to occur.

Age mixing is sometimes a means of matching abilities.

My main concern here has been with the value of play among people with unequal abilities. Before closing, though, I should add that freely chosen play among people with relatively equal abilities is also valuable. In general, children who are similar in age are more similar in abilities than are those who are different in age, but that is not always the case. In an age-mixed environment, a person who is ahead of or behind his or her age-mates in some realm of activity can find equal partners among older or younger children. The child who is awkward at climbing can play at scrambling up rocks and trees with younger children without feeling constantly left behind, and in that way can improve his climbing ability. The talented 11-year-old guitar player, whose musical ability is beyond that of her age-mates, can jam with teenagers who are at her level.

Feldman observed a number of examples of students at Sudbury Valley who were advanced for their age in certain abilities and who frequently played with older children. One example was that of 12-year-old Randy, an excellent chess player, who went to tournaments and had an official ranking. His only chess peers at the school were Jack (age 17), Elana (age 17), and Ken (age 18). All of his serious games, with which he measured his own progress, were with these older students. He might practice new moves in games with his age-mates and younger children, but he tested himself in games with students who were five or six years older than himself.

References

Gray, P. (2008). The value of age-mixed play. *Education Week*, April 16, 2008.

Gray, P. (2011). The special value of age-mixed play. *American Journal of Play*, 3, 500-522.

Gray, P. & Feldman, J. (2004). Playing in the zone of proximal development: Qualities of self-directed age mixing between adolescents and young children at a democratic school. *American Journal of Education*, 110, 108-145.

Greenberg, M. (1992). On the nature of sports at SVS and the limitations of language in describing SVS to the world. In D. Greenberg (Ed.), *The Sudbury Valley School experience*, 3rd ed. Framingham, MA: Sudbury Valley School Press.

6

Why We Should Stop Segregating Children by Age

Part III

Older children are excellent models, helpers, and teachers of younger ones

SEPTEMBER 24, 2008

We adults flatter ourselves when we think that we are the best models, guides, and teachers for children. In fact, children are much more interested in other children than in us. Children are especially interested in, and ready to learn from, those others who are a little older than themselves, a little farther along in their development, but not too far along. Children are drawn to older children, and older children are drawn to adolescents. Adulthood is too far off to be of much concern. That is why age-mixing is crucial to children's self-education.

In the first two essays in this trilogy I focused on the value of age-mixed play. I described how younger children are lifted up in such play to do things that they couldn't do with age-mates; and I described how age-mixed play is often more creative, less competitive, and more conducive to experimentation than is same-age play. Now I complete the series on age mixing by describing some ways, beyond play, by which the presence of older and younger children promotes self-education. As before, my examples come mostly from observations at the Sudbury Valley School, where the students, who range in age from 4 through high-school age, mingle freely all day long.

Younger children want to do what older children do.
One sunny morning as I sat near the school's playground, I watched two 10-year-old girls easily and nonchalantly perform the trick of walking upright down the very tall slide. A 6-year-old girl nearby watched them intently, and then she climbed the ladder and started gingerly walking down the slide herself. This was clearly a challenge for the little girl. She walked with knees bent and hands down, ready to grab the rails if she lost balance. I also noticed that the two older girls remained next to the slide and looked on with a degree of apprehension, ready to catch her, but not too obviously so, if she should fall. One said, "You don't have to do it, you can just slide," but the little girl continued, slowly, and beamed with pride when she made it to the bottom. Shortly after that, the two older girls began climbing a nearby tree, and the younger girl followed them in that activity too. The little girl was clearly motivated to do, with effort, what the older girls could do with ease.

This is just one of dozens of observations we made of young children modeling their behavior after that of older children at the school. Children on the verge of being able to play strategy games, or read, or perform new operations on the computer, or engage in more advanced athletic activities, become motivated to do so by observing those activities in older children and adolescents. In our study of how and why children learn to read at the school, some told us that they wanted to read because they were envious of the older kids who were reading and talking about what they had read. As one student put it, "I wanted the same magic they had; I wanted to join that club."

Younger children don't just blindly mimic older ones. Rather, they watch, think about what they see, and incorporate what they learn into their own behavior in ways that make sense to them. Because of this, even the mistakes and unhealthy behaviors of older children can provide positive lessons for younger ones. Young children talk with one another about what they like and don't like about the activities of the older ones around them. Negative models can be as helpful as positive ones. "I'm not going to do what X does, because I can see all the trouble it brings him."

Children also learn an enormous amount just by listening to or overhearing older ones, even when they aren't interacting with them. Through hearing the language and thoughts of older children—which are more sophisticated than their own, but not so much so as to be out of reach—they expand their own vocabularies and thought.

Older children are also inspired by younger ones.

It is not just the younger children whose horizons are expanded by the age-mixed environment at Sudbury Valley. Older children and teens are inspired by the playthings and actions of younger ones to continue to engage in activities that they probably would have dropped by middle childhood in an age-segregated environment. They continue, for example, to play with blocks, clay, crayons, and paint. As a result, many of them become extraordinarily good at those activities. The school has produced a remarkable number of successful creative artists, and I suspect that the age-mixed environment has much to do with that.

Older children are excellent helpers and advisors of younger children.

Children often prefer to ask an older child rather than an adult for help or advice, even when an adult is available whom they could easily ask. I suspect there are various reasons for this, but one of the main reasons, I think, has to do with control.

Children seeking help or advice do not want to give up their own control of the situation. They don't want any more help than what they ask for, and they want to decide themselves whether or not to accept what is offered. Because adults are more likely to be seen as authority figures than are older children, it is harder to reject an adult's help or walk away when advice goes beyond what the child wants. Moreover, in my observations, older children are much less likely than adults to extend help or advice beyond what the young child wants. Older children are not so concerned about the long-term development of the child who has asked them for help, or about whether or not they are coming across as wonderful teachers and guides, so they just give the help that is asked for, which is all that the younger child wants.

In one of Jay Feldman's observations, for example, 5-year-old Sue asked 8-year-old Anne to thread the needle on a beading loom for her, which she needed to do in order to complete a bracelet she was making (Feldman, 1997). After Anne threaded the needle, Sue continued her work on her own, without further help, and Anne offered none, even though Sue continued to have difficulties with the loom and made many mistakes. If Sue had asked an adult to thread the needle, rather than an older child, the adult might have hovered around and helped Sue with other parts of her project, which would have taken away Sue's pride in doing the work herself. Sue clearly didn't want such further help, even though the project was difficult for her, so it was safer to ask an 8-year-old.

So, here is a valuable lesson that we adults can learn from children about helping and advising children: Don't give more help, or more advice, than is asked for! The same lesson applies to helping and advising adults. I know that when I ask for help, I am not asking for supervision. I just want the help I asked for. I want to do the rest myself, even if I'll make more mistakes that way. A too-helpful helper takes away my sense of freedom, self-control, and play.

Older children are excellent teachers of younger ones.
Daniel Greenberg (1987) made this point in one of his books about Sudbury Valley, where he wrote: "Kids love to learn

from other kids. First of all, it's often easier. The child teacher is closer than an adult to the student's difficulties, having gone through them somewhat more recently. The explanations are usually simpler, better. There's less pressure, less judgment."

Not only are the explanations simpler, but, because they come from someone closer in age, they are easier to challenge. They are more likely to be viewed as ideas to think about, rather than as Truth, and understanding comes from thought, not from blind acceptance. Here is an example from one of Jay Feldman's observations (Gray & Feldman, 2004):

Eight-year-old Ed was complaining to 14-year-old Arthur about how two other boys had been teasing him by calling him names he didn't like. Arthur told Ed that he should bring a complaint to the school's Judicial Committee. Ed then said, "They have freedom of speech." Arthur, after a little thought, replied that freedom of speech meant that they had the right to say those things, but Ed also had the right not to hear them. Ed, after a little thought, said, "Okay."

Notice that in this example Ed felt equal enough to Arthur to challenge his suggestion, and the challenge led to a new idea. Notice also the elegant language of the exchange. Big ideas were expressed in few and simple words.

Older children expand their own understanding through explanations to younger ones.

Everyone who has ever taught knows that we learn more when we teach than when we are taught. The requirement to put ideas into words that others can understand, and the need to think through objections that others might make, lead us to think deeply about what we thought we knew. Often this leads us to a better understanding than we had before. In an age-mixed environment, children, not just adults, can learn through teaching.

In the above example, 14-year-old Arthur, the "teacher," probably learned at least as much as 8-year-old Ed, the protégé, in their conversation. Ed's challenge to Arthur's suggestion led Arthur to think further and expand on his explanation in a way that he may not have thought about previously. Both parties probably left the conversation with a deeper understanding of democracy at the school than they had before.

As another example, consider the case of an older child playing chess or some other strategy game with a younger one and teaching strategy as they play. When the older child says to the younger one that move A would be better than move B, the younger one says, "Why?" To answer this, the experienced player cannot just rely on rote memory or gut instinct developed from long experience with chess but must articulate a reason. She must turn her implicit chess knowledge into conscious, explicit knowledge, and doing so makes her a better chess player. Similar examples occur in every realm of exchange of knowledge and ideas among people who feel free to ask questions.

Older children develop compassion and nurturing skills through helping younger ones.
Even more valuable than the cognitive gains derived from interacting with younger children are the moral gains. To develop effectively as responsible, ethical beings, children need

to have the experience of caring for others, not just the experience of being cared for by others. Observations in many cultures have shown that both boys and girls behave in more caring ways toward children who are several years younger than themselves than toward children near their own age. Little children seem to draw out the nurturing instincts that lie latent in all of us. One study, in Kenya, revealed that boys who cared for younger siblings at home behaved less aggressively, and more kindly, toward same-age peers than did boys who lacked that opportunity (Ember, 1073). Apparently, the nurturing instinct is strengthened through interactions with younger children, and, once strengthened, it generalizes to age-mates.

Many examples of children nurturing younger ones can be seen at Sudbury Valley every day. These include scenes of older children reading to younger ones, who sit on their laps; older children helping younger ones find lost objects or fixing things they have broken; and older children providing all kinds of assistance to younger ones as they go about their daily activities. Some of the most interesting scenes are those in which an older child criticizes a younger one for his or her poor treatment of a still younger child. In one case, for example, we observed a 10-year-old girl explain to three 6-to-8-year-old girls why they should let a certain 4-year-old join them in their game. "How would you feel if you weren't included?" she asked. In another case we observed a 17-year-old boy reprimand a 13-year-old for his unfriendly way of rejecting an 8-year-old boy who asked to play a game with him. The reprimands we heard in these examples appeared to be much more effective coming from an older child than they would have been if they had come from an adult.

Taking this essay along with the previous two, I conclude with the following summary. An age-mixed environment: (a) allows younger children to engage collaboratively in activities that they could not do just with age-mates; (b) promotes non-competitive, creative forms of play that are ideal for acquiring new skills; (c) allows those who are ahead of or behind their age-mates in certain realms to find others who are at their level; (d) permits younger children to be inspired by the activities of older ones, and vice versa; (e) allows younger children to receive help and advice without giving up their own autonomy; (f) allows older children to learn through teaching; and (g) allows older children to practice caring for younger ones and to develop a sense of responsibility and maturity. When we segregate children by age, in schools and in other settings, we deprive them of all of these benefits. We rob them of the opportunity to use fully their natural and joyful ways of learning from one another.

References

Ember, C. R. (1973). Feminine task assignment and the social behavior of boys. *Ethos*, 1, 424-439.

Feldman, J. (1997). The educational opportunities that lie in self-directed age mixing among children and adolescents. Ph.D. dissertation, Department of Psychology, Boston College, 1997.

Gray. P. & Feldman, J. (2004). Playing in the zone of proximal development: Qualities of self-directed age mixing between adolescents and young children at a democratic school. *American Journal of Education*, 110, 108-145.

Greenberg, D. (1987). *Free at last: the Sudbury Valley School*. Framingham, MA: Sudbury Valley School Press.

7

Fighting Bullying with Babies

*Empathy can't be taught, but can
be caught—from babies*

NOVEMBER 24, 2010

We humans are endowed by natural selection (or by God, if you prefer) with contradictory drives and emotions. We are wired to be selfish, mean, and violent; and we are also wired to be generous, compassionate, and loving. The human drama—that runs through all religions, all major accounts of history, and the greatest and truest works of fiction—revolves around this contradictory nature of ours. The devil and the angel are wrapped in a single skin. Our salvation depends on our ability to feed the angel and starve the devil. This is no easy task. There are no sure routes to success. But our greatest assistants in this task may be babies and young children. That is the thesis of this essay.

Look closely at a baby. See its helplessness; feel its pain and joy; experience its faith that someone will care for it and ensure its needs are met. Look at a toddler, acting so bravely, walking and running, experimenting with language, sometimes deliberately being naughty, asserting its independence, and then crying out for Mommy when suddenly frightened. Do this repeatedly and you will find that the compassionate angel in you grows while the mean-spirited devil shrivels. Our species could not have survived more than a generation were it not for our powerful instinct to care for and feel compassion towards babies and young children. And that instinct is transferrable. We can apply it not just to babies and young children, but also to older children, to teenagers, to adults, and—as religious leaders have repeatedly proclaimed—even to those who would be our persecutors and enemies.

A wise woman (my mother) once said to me: "If you want to feel compassion for someone who is really annoying you, imagine that that person is two years old." It works. We are all, in reality, not much different from two-year-olds. We are all, in our own clumsy ways, asserting ourselves in the world, expressing our joys and fears, and calling out for help that we desperately need. It's not hard to look at any human being, even the meanest one, and see the two-year-old.

My essay today was inspired by an article by David Bornstein, posted on the *New York Times* Opinionator blog. Bornstein's article is about the Roots of Empathy program, founded more than a decade ago by Mary Gordon in Toronto. Here I'll say a bit about Gordon's program and then describe some other examples that demonstrate the power of babies and young children to bring out the angel in us and squash the devil.

The Roots of Empathy Program

Mary Gordon founded Roots of Empathy after years of working with abusive parents and abused children. She saw the cycle. Children growing up unloved and surrounded by violence became unloving and violent parents. The idea behind her new program was to bring real babies and their mothers (and sometimes fathers) into school classrooms so that children from all backgrounds could gain some experience of looking at babies, talking about babies, and thinking about what it is like to be a baby. The goal was that this would help set children on the road to becoming, ultimately, better parents.

She found, through experience, that her program also had a remarkable, more immediate effect on the classrooms that participated. The children who had this experience—of a monthly visit from a baby and parent—became kinder and more compassionate with one another. Bullying declined. Kids who were previously teased and taunted for being different were now in many cases admired for their differences. Apparently, the exposure to the infant, and the discussions of the thoughts and feelings that the infant evoked, served as a powerful force for the spread of compassion throughout the classroom—an effect that would last the whole month, from one baby visit to the next.

Here is a sample story from Gordon's (2005) book about her program. In one eighth-grade class, the toughest and meanest-looking kid was Darren. He was two years older than the others because he had been held back. He was al-

ready growing a beard, had a tattoo on the back of his par-
tially shaved head, and was intimidating to all around him.
Darren's mother had been murdered in front of his eyes when
he was four years old, and he had lived in a series of foster
homes. So, he had to look and act tough. But a 6-month-old
baby who had been brought to the classroom melted him.

The mom had brought along a Snuggly, trimmed with
pink brocade, which she used for holding the baby close to
her. Near the end of the class visit—after the class had spent
40 minutes observing and talking about the baby—the
mother asked if anyone would like to try on the Snuggly. To
everyone's dismay, Darren raised his hand. With the Snuggly strapped on, he then asked the mom if she would put the
baby into it. With some apprehension, the mother did just
that. Darren then sat quietly for several minutes in the corner
rocking, while the baby snuggled contentedly into his arms
and chest. When it was time for the baby and mother to leave,
Darren asked the mother and the instructor: "If a person has
never been loved, can he still be a good father?"

The Roots of Empathy program has now spread throughout Canada and made inroads into a number of other countries. Kimberly Schonert-Reichl, a psychology professor at
the University of British Columbia, has conducted controlled
studies which show that the program reduces aggression and
increases kindness not just on the day of the baby's visit, but
throughout the school year (Schoenert-Reichl et al., 2012).
Mary Gordon likes to say, "Empathy can't be taught, but it
can be caught. You catch it from babies."

Pastor Daniel Dean and the HOPE
Community Center and School in Tampa

I met Daniel Dean two months prior to writing this essay, at a symposium on the value of free play that I helped to organize in Binghamton, New York. He was brought to the symposium by Jerry Lieberman, who is president of the Florida Humanist Society. Jerry wanted my academic colleagues and me to meet Daniel and learn from him, and Daniel himself came with the hope of learning something from us. I don't know if Daniel learned anything worth knowing from us, but I certainly learned much from him.

Daniel Dean, who was born in Jamaica but grew up in Florida, is a Christian pastor and community leader. He and volunteers built, from scratch, a community center on North 22nd Street in Tampa, at a corner long known for drug dealing, prostitution, and violence. The mayor of Tampa had offered a vacant lot on this corner to anyone who would create something there that would help to improve the neighborhood, and Daniel took up the challenge. He and his wife Suzette, along with other volunteers, built a center that would house a church on Sundays, a daycare and school on weekdays, and a community and recreation center for people of all ages, on weekday evenings and at other times when school wasn't in session. Some people thought he was crazy. The place would be vandalized, destroyed before the roof went up. And if the roof did go up and children came, the children would be in constant danger from the "element" surrounding it. But Daniel thought differently, and so far he has been proven correct.

As Daniel worked at constructing the building, often with his two young sons working by his side, people from the neighborhood came over to ask about what he was doing and why. They were proud of his project, moved by his respectful relationship with his boys, and pleased to volunteer to help. Daniel also made a point of getting to know the people hanging around the bar across the street. They, too, were emotionally moved by the idea that a school for little children, as well as a community center for people of all ages, was being built right there, across the street from the bar. Daniel clearly trusted them, and trust breeds trustworthiness. Even before the center was completed, the fighting outside that bar stopped and the drug dealers and prostitutes started drifting away. Apparently, such activities were incompatible with the feelings evoked by the thought of a center for little children across the street.

The building was completed more than a year prior to my writing this, and the school and community center are in full swing. The center is called HOPE (for Helping Our People Excel). The school at the time of my writing had 80 students, ranging from one-year-old infants up through high-school students. Most are from families that are close to or below the poverty line. In the evening, adults as well as children come to play checkers and chess, use the computers, take classes (such as a cooking class), obtain help in finding employment, hold meetings, and socialize. They bring their babies and toddlers along, and the kids of all ages play in age-mixed groups.

According to Daniel, the violence and vandalism on the street have stopped and there has been no violence or vandalism at all in the school. The people feel that this fine school and center are theirs, and they are proud of it, and nobody is going to destroy it. The sense of community ownership is a big part of the success, but I think that the more-or-less continuous presence of little children plays an equally big role. Daniel agrees.

According to Daniel Dean, every day at the school starts with an age-mixed recess. The kids play together and get to know everyone, of all ages. The older ones naturally develop big-brother, big-sister relationships with the little ones, and the sense of caring expands outward to encompass everyone in the school and, perhaps, beyond.

Cross-Cultural Evidence for the Pacifying Power of Babies and Young Children

In a review of research on children's social interactions conducted in many different cultures, anthropologist Beatrice Whiting (1983) concluded that boys and girls everywhere demonstrate more kindness and compassion in interactions with children who are at least three years younger than themselves than they do toward children closer to their own age. She suggested that interactions with younger children and babies are the vehicle through which children and teenagers exercise and develop their capacities to nurture others, and that these capacities, as they develop, may generalize to interactions with people of all ages.

Consistent with this theory, anthropologist Carol Ember (1973) reported on a study that she conducted of boys, in the age range of 8 to 16, in a subsistence farming community in Kenya. In this community, girls were expected to help their mothers care for younger children and infants at home, but in families where there were no girls of the appropriate age, boys were required to do this task. Ember reported that boys who were regular babysitters at home were, on average, kinder, more helpful, and less aggressive in their interactions with their own peers than were boys who did not have such babysitting experience.

How Young Children Promote Kindness at the Sudbury Valley School

At the Sudbury Valley School, students from age 4 on through high-school age are free to explore and play as they wish, with whom they wish, all day long. In our research, Jay Feldman and I documented many ways in which children and adolescents at the school regularly practice their nurturing skills through self-chosen interactions with younger children (Feldman & Gray, 2004). They read to them, comfort them, correct them when they violate rules, teach them games, help them do things that they cannot do alone, help them find lost objects, and take pride in their accomplishments. They are, I think, on their own initiatives practicing to be parents; and, more generally, they are practicing the kinds of abilities that will make them caring and valuable helpers and leaders to everyone around them.

It is sad to see, in our age-segregated society, that many if not most children and adolescents have few opportunities to get to know and to interact regularly with children who are much younger than themselves. If we want young people to grow up to be compassionate and caring, we need to allow them to exercise those capacities; and to do that we need to break down the barriers we have erected to keep young people of different ages apart. We are designed by nature to learn to be compassionate by observing and caring for younger children while we ourselves are growing up.

References

Ember, R. C. (1973). Feminine task assignment and the social behavior of boys. *Ethos*, 1, 424-439.

Gordon, M. (2005). *Roots of empathy*. Toronto: Thomas Allen Publishers.

Gray, P. & Feldman, J. (2004). Playing in zone of proximal development: Qualities of self-directed age mixing between adolescents and young children at a democratic school. *American Journal of Education*, 110, 108-145.

Schonert-Reichl, K. A., Smith, V., Zaidman-Zait, A., & Hertzman, C. (2012). Promoting children's prosocial behaviors in school: Impact of the "Roots of Empathy" program on the social and emotional competence of school-aged children. *School Mental Health*, 4, 1-21.

Whiting, B. B. (1983). The genesis of prosocial behavior. In: D. L. Bridgeman (Ed.), *The nature of prosocial development: interdisciplinary theories and strategies*. New York: Academic Press.

8

The Human Nature of Teaching
What Can We Learn from Hunter-Gatherers?

How hunter-gatherers taught without coercion

MAY 2, 2011

In a previous essay, I defined teaching, very broadly, as behavior that is conducted by one individual (the teacher) for the purpose of helping another individual (the pupil) to learn something (Gray, 2011). I presented examples showing that, by this definition, teaching can be found even among non-human animals. Now I wish to examine teaching as it occurs, or occurred, in hunter-gatherer bands.

All humans were hunter-gatherers until a mere 10,000 years ago, when agriculture first appeared in some parts of the planet. In other words, for about 99% of our million or so years on earth (more or less, depending on just how you want to define "human beings") we were all hunter-gatherers. Our basic human instincts, including our instincts to learn and to teach, were shaped to meet the needs of our hunter-gatherer way of life. We know a good deal about that way of life through studies of those groups of people, in various isolated parts of the world, who managed to survive as hunter-gatherers into the last half of the 20th century and were studied by anthropologists. Wherever they were found, these people lived in small bands, of roughly 20 to 50 people per band, that moved from campsite to campsite to follow the available game and edible vegetation. They had rich cultures, and children had to learn a lot to become effective adults, but they learned it through their own self-initiated activities (Gray, 2009).

Hunter-gatherers everywhere had faith that their children would, in their own ways, learn what they needed to know and so they did not worry about their children's education or attempt to control it. Moreover, hunter-gatherers held strongly to the values of personal autonomy and equality. They believed that it is wrong for anyone to try to control another person's life, either in the short run or the long run, even if that other person is a child. They believed that it is presumptuous for anyone to think that they know what is best for another person. So, they did not "teach" in the sense of trying to get their children to do things that the children were not already motivated to do. But they did teach by my broad definition of teaching. They deliberately behaved in ways that were designed to help their children learn what the children wanted to learn. Here are the major categories of ways by which adult hunter-gatherers helped their children learn.

Providing Children with Ample Time to Play and Explore

Hunter-gatherer children were the freest human children ever to have walked the earth. Hunter-gathers believed that children learn through their own, self-directed, self-initiated play and exploration, so they allowed their children unlimited time for such activities. In a survey of hunter-gatherer researchers that I helped to conduct some years ago, all said that the children in the group that they had studied were free to explore on their own, without adult guidance, essentially from dawn to dusk every day (Gray, 2009, 2012). They were allowed such freedom beginning at about age 4 (the age at which, according to hunter-gathers, children "have sense" and do not need to be watched regularly by adults) and continuing into their mid to late teenage years, when they began to take on adult responsibilities. By providing children with food and other subsistence needs, and by not burdening them with many chores, hunter-gatherer adults allowed their children ample time to educate themselves.

Providing Children with the Culture's Tools

In order to learn to use the tools of the culture, children must have access to those tools and be allowed to play with them. Hunter-gatherers recognized that, and they allowed their children nearly unlimited opportunities to play with the tools of their culture, even dangerous ones such as knives and axes. (There were some limits, however; the poison-tipped darts or arrows that adults used for hunting were kept well out of small children's reach.) The adults also made scaled-down versions of tools—such as small bows and arrows, digging sticks, and baskets—specifically for young children, even toddlers, to play with. Providing children with playthings is one means of teaching that is common to our culture and hunter-gatherer cultures. However, hunter-gatherers were more likely than we are to allow their children to play with the real versions of the culture's tools, not pretend ones. Even the scaled-down tools were real; the small bows, arrows, axes, and digging sticks functioned just like the bigger versions.

Allowing Children to Observe and Participate in Adult Activities

Hunter-gatherer adults recognized that children learn by watching, listening, and participating, and so they did not exclude children from adult activities. By all accounts, they were enormously tolerant of children's interruptions, and they allowed children into their workspaces even when that meant the work would proceed more slowly. On their own initiatives, children often joined their mothers on gathering trips, where they learned by watching and sometimes helping. By the time they were young teenagers, boys who were eager to do so were allowed to join men on big-game hunting expeditions, so they could watch and learn. By the time they were in their middle teens, they were actively contributing to, rather than detracting from, the success of such trips. Within a few years after that, they were full-fledged hunters.

In camp, children often crowded around adults, and young ones climbed onto adults' laps, to watch or "help" them cook, or make hunting weapons and other tools, or play musical instruments, or make beaded decorations; and the adults rarely shooed them away. As illustration of the adults' tolerance of children's interruptions of their activities, here is a typical scene described by anthropologist Patricia Draper (1976, pp 205-206):

> "One afternoon I watched for 2 hours while a [Ju/'hoan] father hammered and shaped the metal for several arrow points. During the period his son and grandson (both under 4 years old) jostled him, sat on his legs, and attempted to pull the arrowheads from under the hammer. When the boys' fingers came close to the point of impact, he merely waited until the small hands were a little farther away before he resumed hammering. Although the man remonstrated with the boys, he did not become cross or chase the boys off; and they did not heed his warnings to quit interfering. Eventually, perhaps 50 minutes later, the boys moved off a few steps to join some teenagers lying in the shade."

Showing How, or Providing Information

When children asked adults to show them how to do something or to help them do it, the adults obliged. As one group of hunter-gatherer researchers (Hewlett et al., 2011) put it, "Sharing and giving are core forager values, so what an individual knows is open and available to everyone; if a child wants to learn something, others are obliged to share the knowledge or skill." In the course of natural daily life, an adult might show a child the best way to swing an axe or might point out the difference between the footprints of two different, closely related mammals—but only if the child wanted such help. In an interview study, hunter-gather women (of the Aka culture) described how, when they were young, their mothers had placed varieties of mushrooms or wild yams in front of them and explained the differences between those that were edible and those that were not (Hewlett et al., 2011).

Another source for learning were the stories told—by men about their hunting trips, by women about their gathering trips, by both men and women about their visits to other bands, and, especially, by the older members of the band about significant events in the past. Elizabeth Marshall Thomas (2006), who was one of the first to study the Ju/'hoan hunter-gatherers of the Kalahari Desert, noted that women in their sixties and seventies were especially great storytellers. The stories were not directed specifically to children, but the children listened and absorbed the meaning. My guess is that the fact that the stories were directed to everyone, not specifically to children, made them all the more interesting and memorable to the children.

Exercising Children's Natural
Desires to Share and Give

Research in our culture has shown that infants as young as 12 months old, delight in giving things to other people. In a series of little-known experiments conducted in the United States, nearly every one of more than 100 infants, aged 12 to 18 months, spontaneously gave toys to an adult during brief sessions in a laboratory room (Hay & Murray, 1982). In our culture, such joyful and voluntary giving by infants is not much commented upon, but in at least some hunter-gatherer cultures it was celebrated, much like the earliest words of infants are celebrated in our culture. In various ways, hunter-gatherer adults cultivated the giving instincts of infants and young children. For example, toddlers were invited to participate in the band's food sharing, by carrying food from one hut to another, which they did with great delight.

Among the Ju/'hoansi, grandmothers took special responsibility to initiate infants into the culture of sharing by playing games of give and take with them and by encouraging games in which infants would pass beads and other valued objects to others in the band (Bakeman et al., 1990; Wiessner, 1982). This is the one example of systematic, deliberate adult influence on children's play that I have found in the hunter-gatherer research literature. No human trait was more crucial to the hunter-gatherer way of life than the willingness to give or share. Their survival depended on it (and so, really, does ours, if we stop to think about it).

Providing a Trustful Social Environment
within which to Learn

The most important and general way by which hunter-gatherer adults helped their children learn was to provide a consistently supportive, trustful environment. To educate themselves, children need to feel emotionally secure and confident. By trusting children to know what is best for themselves and by making that trust apparent, adult hunter-gatherers provided the conditions that all children need in order to feel confident about taking control of their own lives and learning. Because all adult members of the band cared about and provided for the emotional and physical needs of all the children, and because it was a cultural taboo to deliberately hurt a child, the children grew up feeling that others were trustworthy, which is a prerequisite for becoming trustworthy oneself. In such an environment, children's instincts for self-education flourish. That is as true today as it ever was, as is regularly observed at the Sudbury Valley School.

The secure child, raised in a setting where others are loving, trusting, and nonjudgmental, and where the tools and examples needed for education are available but not forced upon anyone, vigorously and joyfully undertakes the natural childhood task of self-education. Unfortunately, in our conventional schools, we replace security with anxiety as the foundation for learning, and we keep children so busy doing what they are told to do that self-education becomes essentially impossible. In schools we "teach" in ways that subvert children's natural instincts to learn and that replace trust and security with distrust and anxiety.

References

Bakeman, R., Adamson, L. B., Konner, M., & Barr, R. (1990). !Kung infancy: The social context of object exploration. *Child Development*, 61, 794-809.

Gray, P. (2009). Play as the foundation for hunter-gatherer social existence. *American Journal of Play*, 1, 476-522. 2009.

Draper, P. (1976). Social and economic constraints on child life among the !Kung. In R. B. Lee & I. DeVore (Eds.), *Kalahari hunter-gatherers: studies of the !Kung San and their neighbors*, pp. 199-217. Cambridge, MA: Harvard University Press., p 205-206.

Gray, P. (2011). The human nature of teaching I: Ways of teaching that we share with other animals. *Psychology Today*. Online at https://www.psychologytoday.com/intl/blog/freedom-learn/201104/
the-human-nature-teaching-i-ways-teaching-we-share-other-animals.

Gray, P. (2012). The value of a play-filled childhood in development of the hunter-gatherer individual. In Narvaez, D., Panksepp, J., Schore, A., & Gleason, T. (Eds.), *Evolution, Early Experience and Human Development: From Research to Practice and Policy*, pp 252-370. New York: Oxford University Press,

Hay, D. F., & Murray, P. (1982). Giving and requesting: Social facilitation of infants' offers to adults. *Infant Behavior and Development*, 5, 301-310.

Hewlett, B. S., Fouts, H. N., Boyette, A., & Hewlett, B. L. (2011). Social learning among Congo Basin hunter-gatherers. *Philosophical Transactions of the Royal Society B*, 366, 1168-1178.

Thomas, E. M. (2006). The old way. New York: Farrar, Straus & Giroux.

Wiessner, P. (1982). Risk, reciprocity and social influences on !Kung San economics. In E. Leacock & R. Lee (Eds.), *Politics and history in band societies*. Cambridge, UK: Cambridge University Press.

9

The Joy and Sorrow of Rereading
Holt's *How Children Learn*

*A summary of John Holt's great
insights about children's learning*

DECEMBER 26, 2017

In a survey conducted a few years ago, Gina Riley and I asked unschooling families to name the writers whose works had influenced them most in their decision to take that route. John Holt was by far the most often cited, named by more than half of the 232 families in the survey (Gray & Riley, 2013). Holt died in 1985, of cancer at the too-young age of 62. Yet he continues to exert great influence.

My colleague Pat Farenga, who has managed Holt's legacy ever since his death, recently oversaw the publication of the 50th anniversary edition of what to me is Holt's most significant book, *How Children Learn* (Da Capo Press, 2017). I read the first edition decades ago, without full appreciation, before I had begun my own research into children's learning.

Rereading the book now led me repeatedly to think, "How true, how brilliant, how sad." Sad because these truths and insights are still understood by only a small percentage of the population, and our schools are now even worse than they were when Holt was alive. They are even more anxiety provoking, more wasteful of young people's time, more insulting of young people's intelligence, and more disruptive of deep learning and understanding.

But yet I am optimistic, as I think Holt might be if he were alive today, because even though the percentage of people who understand that children learn best when allowed to control their own learning remains small, that percentage is growing. It is reflected in the ever-increasing number of families who are choosing to take their children out of standard schools and opting instead for Self-Directed Education or something close to it. A growing number of parents are seeing the light of children's brilliance and are choosing to allow it to shine. Eventually, I think, we will reach a tipping point where the rate of school leaving accelerates sharply. Then what we now call standard schooling will die of irrelevance, replaced by centers designed to optimize children's natural ways of learning.

Some of Holt's Insights into Children's Learning

Holt was an astute and brilliant observer of children. If he had studied some species of animal, instead of human children, we would call him a naturalist. He observed children in their natural, free condition, where they were not being controlled by a teacher in a classroom or an experimenter in a laboratory. This is something that far too few developmental psychologists or educational researchers have done. He observed the children of his relatives and friends when they were playing and exploring, and he observed children in schools during breaks in their formal lessons. Through such observations, he came to certain profound conclusions about children's learning. Here is a summary of them, which I extracted from the pages of *How Children Learn*.

Children don't choose to learn in order to do things in the future. They choose to do right now what others in their world do, and through doing they learn.

Schools try to teach children skills and knowledge that may benefit them at some unknown time in the future. But children are interested in the present, not the future. They want to do real things now. By doing what they want to do they also prepare themselves wonderfully for the future, but that is a side effect. This, I think, is the main insight of the book; most of the other ideas are more or less corollaries.

Children are brilliant learners because they don't think of themselves as learning; they think of themselves as doing. They want to engage in whole, meaningful activities, like the activities they see around them, and they aren't afraid to try. They want to walk, like other people do, but at first they aren't good at it. So they keep trying, day after day, and their walking keeps getting better. They want to talk, like other people do, but at first they don't know about the relationships of sounds to meanings. Their sentences come across to us as babbled nonsense, but in the child's mind he or she is talking (as Holt suggests, on p 75). Improvement comes because the child attends to others' talking, gradually picks up some of the repeated sounds and their meanings, and works them into his or her own utterances in increasingly appropriate ways.

As children grow older they continue to attend to activities around them and, in unpredictable ways at unpredictable times, choose those that they want to do and start doing them. Children start reading because they see that others read, and if they are read to they discover that reading is a route to the enjoyment of stories. Children don't become readers by first learning to read; they start right off by reading. They may read signs, which they recognize. They may recite, verbatim, the words in a little book they have memorized, as they turn the pages; or they may turn the pages of an unfamiliar book and say whatever comes to mind. We may not call that reading, but to the child it is reading. Over time, the child begins to recognize certain words, even in new contexts, and begins to infer the relationships between letters and sounds. In this way, the child's reading improves.

Walking, talking, and reading are skills that nearly everyone picks up in our culture because they are so prevalent. Other skills are picked up more selectively, by those who somehow become fascinated by them. Holt gives an example of a six-year-old girl who became interested in typing with an electric typewriter (this was the 1960s). She would type fast, like the adults in her family, but without attention to the fact that the letters on the page were random. She would produce whole documents this way. Over time she began to be concerned that her documents differed from those of adults in that they were not readable, and then she began to pay attention to which keys she would strike and to the effect this had on the sheet of paper. She began to type very carefully rather than fast. Before long she was typing out readable statements.

You and I might say that the child is learning to walk, talk, read, or type; but from the child's view that would be wrong. The child is walking with the very first step, talking with the first babbled utterance, reading with the first recognition of "stop" on a sign, and typing with the first striking of keys. The child isn't learning to do these things; he or she is doing them, right from the beginning, and in the process is getting better at them. My colleague Kerry McDonald (2017) made this point very well in an essay about her young unschooled daughter who loves to bake. In Kerry's words, "When people ask her what she wants to be when she grows up, she responds breezily, 'A baker, but I already am one.'"

Children go from whole to parts in their learning, not from parts to whole.

This clearly is a corollary of the point that children learn because they are motivated to do the things they see others do. They are motivated to do whole things, not pieces abstracted out of the whole. They are motivated to speak meaningful sentences, not phonemes. Nobody speaks phonemes. They are motivated to read interesting stories, not memorize grapheme-phoneme relationships or be drilled on sight words. As Holt points out repeatedly, one of our biggest mistakes in schools is to break tasks down into components and try to get children to practice the components isolated from the whole. In doing so we turn what would be meaningful and exciting into something meaningless and boring. Children pick up the components (e.g., grapheme-phoneme relationships) naturally, incidentally, as they go along in their exciting work of doing things that are real, meaningful, and whole.

Children learn by making mistakes and then noticing and correcting their own mistakes.

Children are motivated not just to do what they see others do, but to do those things well. They are not afraid to do what they cannot yet do well, but they are not blind to the mismatches between their own performance and that of the experts they see around them. So, they start right off doing, and then go on to work at improving. In Holt's words (p 34), "Very young children seem to have what could be called an instinct of Workmanship. We tend not to see it, because they are unskillful and their materials are crude. But watch the loving care with which a little child smooths off a sand cake or pats and shapes a mud pie." And later (p 198), "When they are not bribed or bullied, they want to do whatever they are doing better than they did it before."

We adults have a strong tendency to correct children, to point out their mistakes, in the belief that we are helping them learn. But when we do this, according to Holt, we are in effect belittling the child, telling the child that he or she isn't doing it right and we can do it better. We are causing the child to feel judged, and therefore anxious, thereby taking away some of his or her fearlessness about trying this or any other new activity. We may be causing the child to turn away from the very activity that we wanted to support. When children first start an activity they should not be worried about making mistakes, because to do so would make it impossible to start. Only they knows when they are ready to attend to mistakes and make corrections.

Holt points out that we don't need to correct children, because they are very good at correcting themselves. They are continually trying to improve what they do, on their own schedules, in their own ways. As illustration, Holt described his observation of a little girl misreading certain words as she read a story aloud, but then she corrected her own mistakes in subsequent re-readings, as she figured out what made sense and what didn't. In Holt's words (p 140), "Left alone, not hurried, not made anxious, she was able to find and correct most of the mistakes herself."

Children may learn better by watching older children than by watching adults.

Holt points out that young children are well aware of the ways that they are not as competent as the adults around them, and this can be a source of shame and anxiety, even if the adults don't draw attention to it. He writes (p 123), "Parents who do everything well may not always be good examples for their children; sometimes such children feel, since they can never hope to be as good as their parents, there is no use in even trying." This, he says, is why children may learn better by watching somewhat older children than by watching adults. As one example, he describes (p 182) how young boys naturally and efficiently improved their softball skills by observing somewhat older and more experienced boys, who were better than they but not so much better as to be out of reach. This observation fits very well with findings from my research on the value of age-mixed play (Gray, 2011).

Fantasy provides children the means to do and learn from activities that they cannot yet do in reality.

A number of psychologists, myself included, have written about the cognitive value of fantasy, how it underlies the highest form of human thinking: hypothetical reasoning. But Holt brings us another insight about fantasy; it provides a means of "doing" what the child cannot do in reality. In his discussion of fantasy, Holt criticizes the view, held by Maria Montessori and some of her followers, that fantasy should be discouraged in children because it is an escape from reality. Holt, in contrast, writes (p 228), "Children use fantasy not to get out of, but to get into, the real world."

A little child can't really drive a truck, but in fantasy he can be a truck driver. Through such fantasy he can learn a lot about trucks and even something about driving one as he makes his toy truck imitate what real trucks do. Holt points out that children playing fantasy games often choose roles that exist in the adult world around them. They pretend to be mommies or daddies, truck drivers, train conductors, pilots, doctors, teachers, police officers, or the like. In their play they model, as close as they can, their understanding of what adults in those roles do. I have learned from anthropologists that such fantasy is normal for children everywhere. For example, young hunter-gatherer boys imagine themselves to be courageous, big-game hunters as they stalk butterflies or small rodents and try to hit them with their small arrows. They are practicing what it feels like to be a hunter, and they are also developing real hunting skills. This experience is much more exciting than, say, engaging in target practice.

This point about fantasy is another elaboration of Holt's thesis that children learn by doing what they want to do right now, not by practicing for the future. In fantasy, the child can, right now, do things that nature or authority won't permit him or her to do in reality.

Children make sense of the world by creating mental models and assimilating new information to those models.
As children interact with the world their minds are continually active. They are trying to make sense of things. Holt points out, as have others (including, most famously, Piaget), that children are truly scientists, developing hunches (hypotheses) and then testing those hunches and accepting, modifying, or rejecting them based on experience. But the motivation must come from within the child; it can't be imposed. As illustration, Holt describes cases where children who were allowed to just "mess around" with balance beams and pendulums, when they wanted to, learned much more, in a lasting way, about the natural laws of balance and pendulum action than those who were taught explicitly.

Children often use mental models that they developed from previous activities to help them make sense of new activities. Holt gives a wonderful example of a boy who loved trains and knew a lot about them. When this boy began to get interested in reading he noticed that a printed sentence is like a train, with a front end and a back end, going in a certain direction. He called the capital letter at the beginning the "engine" and the period at the end the "caboose." This model, of course, was one that was uniquely useful to this boy. Among other things, it helped him transfer his love of trains into a love of reading. But the model had to come from the boy himself. If a teacher had imposed it on him, it would probably have come across to him as artificial and would have subverted his own attempt to make sense of sentences. And if a teacher tried to use this analogy between a sentence and a train in teaching children who had no particular interest in trains, that would be even more artificial and ineffective.

How Teaching Interferes with Children's Learning

When Holt wrote the first edition of *How Children Learn* (published in 1967), he was still trying to figure out how to become a better teacher. When he revised the book for the second edition (published in 1983) he inserted many corrections, which revealed his growing belief that teaching of any sort is usually a mistake, except in response to a student's explicit request for help. Here, for example, is one of his 1983 insertions (p 112): "When we teach without being asked we are saying in effect, 'You're not smart enough to know that you should know this, and not smart enough to learn it.'" A few pages later (p 126), he inserted, "The spirit of independence in learning is one of the most valuable assets a learner can have, and we who want to help children's learning at home or in school, must learn to respect and encourage it."

Children naturally resist being taught because it undermines their independence and their confidence in their own abilities to figure things out and to ask for help, themselves, when they need it. Moreover, no teacher—certainly not one in a classroom of more than a few children—can get into each child's head and understand that child's motives, mental models, and passions at the time. Only the child has access to all of this, which is why children learn best when they are allowed complete control of their own learning. Or, as the child would say, when they are allowed complete control of their own doing.

References

Gray, P. (2011). The special value of age-mixed play. *American Journal of Play*, 3, 500-522.

McDonald, K. (2017). What do you want to be when you grow up? Whole Family Learning Blog. http://www.wholefamilylearning.com/2017/11/what-do-you-want-to-be-when-you-grow-up.html

10

Toddlers Want to Help and
We Should Let Them

If allowed to help, toddlers become
great work partners later in childhood

SEPTEMBER 25, 2018

We, in the United States and many other Western nations, are more likely to think of children as sources of extra work than as sources of help. We tend to think that trying to get our children to help us at home or elsewhere is more effort than it is worth. We also tend to think that the only way to get children to help is to pressure them through punishment or bribery, which, for good reasons, we may be loath to do. We ourselves generally think of work as something that people naturally don't want to do, and we pass that view on to our children, who then pass it on to their children.

But researchers have found strong evidence that very young children innately want to help, and if allowed to do so

will continue helping, voluntarily, through the rest of childhood and into adulthood. Here is some of that evidence.

Evidence of Toddlers' Instinct to Help

In a classic research study conducted more than 35 years ago,
Harriet Rheingold (1982) observed children ages 18, 24, and
30 months interacting with their parent (mother in some
cases, father in others) as the parent went about doing routine housework, such as folding laundry, dusting, sweeping
the floor, clearing dishes off the table, and putting away items
scattered on the floor. For the sake of the study, each parent
was asked to work relatively slowly and allow their child to
help if the child wanted, but not to ask the child to help or
direct the child's help through verbal instructions. The result
was that all of these young children—80 in all—voluntarily
helped do the work. Most of them helped with more than half
of the tasks that the parent undertook, and some even began
tasks before the parent got to them. Moreover, in Rheingold's
words, "The children carried out their efforts with quick and
energetic movement, excited vocal intonations, animated
facial expressions, and with delight in the finished task."

Many other studies have confirmed this apparently universal desire of toddlers to help. A common procedure is to
bring the little child into the laboratory, allow him or her to
play with toys in one part of the room, and then create a condition in which the experimenter needs help in another part
of the room. For example, the experimenter might "acciden-
tally" drop something onto the floor, over a barrier, and try

but fail to reach it. The child, who is on the other side of the barrier from the experimenter, can help by picking the object up and handing it over the barrier to the experimenter. The key question is: Does the child come over and help without being asked? The answer is yes, in almost every case. All the experimenter has to do is draw attention to the fact, through a grunt and attempts to reach over the barrier, that she is trying to get the object. Even infants as young as 14 months have been found regularly to help in these situations (Warneken & Tomasello, 2009). They see what the experimenter is trying to do, infer what she needs, and then, on their own initiative, satisfy that need.

This helping is not done for some expected reward. In fact, Felix Warneken and Michael Tomasello (2008) found that giving a reward for helping reduces subsequent helping. In one experiment, they allowed 20-month-old children to help an experimenter in a variety of ways and either rewarded the child (with an opportunity to play with an attractive toy) or not. Then they tested the children with more opportunities to help, where no reward was offered. The result was that those who had been previously rewarded for helping were now much less likely to help than those who had not been rewarded. Only 53% of the children in the previously rewarded condition helped, in this test, compared with 89% in the unrewarded condition.

This finding is evidence that children are intrinsically motivated rather than extrinsically motivated to help—that is, they help because they want to be helpful, not because they expect to get something for it. Much other research has shown that rewards tend to undermine intrinsic motivation. For example, in one classic study, children who were rewarded for drawing a picture subsequently engaged in much less drawing than children who had not been rewarded for drawing (Lepper, Greene, & Nisbett, 1973). Rewards apparently change people's attitudes about a previously enjoyed activity, from something that one does for its own sake to something that one does primarily to get a reward. This occurs for adults as well as for children (Deci, Koestner & Ryan, 1999).

We parents, in our culture, tend to make two mistakes regarding our little children's desires to help. First, we brush their offers to help aside, because we are in a rush to get things done and believe (often correctly) that the toddler's "help" will slow us down or the toddler won't do it right and we will have to do it over again. Second, if we do actually want help from the child, we offer some sort of deal, some reward, for doing it. In the first case, we present the message to the child that he or she is not capable of helping; and in the second case, we present the message that helping is something a person will do only if they get something in return.

Cross-Cultural Evidence that Toddlers Who Are Allowed to Help Become Truly Helpful Later in Childhood

Researchers studying various Indigenous communities and Indigenous-heritage communities (communities not far removed from Indigenous ways) have found that parents in those communities respond positively to the desires of their toddlers to help, even when the "help" slows them down, because they believe that this pleases the child and helps the child learn to become a truly valuable helper. The research also shows that, by the time they are about 5 or 6 years old, children in those communities are very effective, willing helpers. Actually, "helper" is not even the correct word here. A better word is "partner," because they act as if the family's work is as much their responsibility as it is their parents'.

Illustrations of this can be found, for example, in a study in which researchers interviewed mothers of 6- to 8-year-olds in Guadalajara, Mexico (Alcala, Rogoff, Mejia-Arauz, Coppens, & Dexter, 2014). Nineteen of the mothers were from an Indigenous-heritage community, still rather closely linked to their Native American roots, and the other 14 were from a more cosmopolitan, Westernized urban community. All of the children attended school, but the parents in the Indigenous-heritage community had much less schooling than those in the cosmopolitan community. The research revealed great differences in ways that the two sets of parents described their children's contributions to household tasks. According to the parents' reports, 74% of the children in the Indigenous-heritage community regularly took initiative in family household work, without being asked, compared with none of the children in the cosmopolitan community. For illustration, here are quotes from two of the Indigenous-heritage mothers describing their children's activities:

"There are days when she comes home and says: 'Mom, I'm going to help you do everything.' Then she picks up the entire house, voluntarily. Or sometimes, when I'm not done cleaning the house, she tells me, 'Mom you've come home really tired, let's start cleaning the house.' And then she turns the radio on and tells me, 'You do one thing, and I'll do something else,' and I clean the kitchen and she picks up the rooms."

"Everybody knows what they need to do, and without having to ask her, she tells me, 'Mommy I just got home from school, I'm going to visit my grandma, but before I go, I'm going to finish my work,' and she finishes and then she goes."

In contrast, the cosmopolitan mothers reported very little voluntary helping from their children and seemed to denigrate what little help a child did offer. Here, for example, is a quotation from one of these mothers: "I'll walk into the bathroom and everything is all soapy, and she says to me 'I'm just cleaning.' I tell her, 'You know what? It's better that you don't clean anything for me because I'm going to slip and fall in here.'"

All in all, the Indigenous-heritage mothers described their children as capable, autonomous, self-initiating, willing partners while the cosmopolitan mothers described their children as subordinates who generally helped only begrudgingly and needed to be told what to do. In the researchers' words, "Most mothers (87%) in the Indigenous-heritage community reported that their children planned and chose their 'free-time' activities (work, unstructured play, homework, religious classes, and visiting relatives and friends), compared with only two mothers (16%) in the cosmopolitan community." Indeed, other studies, involving first-hand observations of the children in their homes, confirm these parents' reports.

To many people in our culture, it may seem counterintuitive that children who were most free to choose their own activities, and therefore the least directed by their parents, were the children who contributed most to the family's welfare.

Anthropologists have described children's universal, natural drive to learn by observing others around them and then trying out for themselves the activities they observe (Lancy, Bock, & Gaskins, 2010). Cross-cultural researcher Barbara Rogoff has described this mode of self-directed education as Learning by Observing and Pitching In, or LOPI (Rogoff, Mejia-Arauz, & Correa Chavez, 2015). Helping with housework is just one example of LOPI.

A How-To Summary

In sum, the research I've described here suggests that, if you want your child to be a partner with you in taking responsibility for the family work, you should do the following:

- Assume it *is* the family work, and not just your work, which means not only that you are not the only person responsible to get it done, but also that you must relinquish some of the control over how it is done. If you want it done exactly your way, you will either have to do it yourself or hire someone to do it.

- Assume that your toddler's attempts to help are genuine and that, if you take the time to let the toddler help, with perhaps just a bit of cheerful guidance, he or she will eventually become good at it.

- Avoid demanding help, or bargaining for it, or rewarding it, or micromanaging it, as all of that undermines the child's intrinsic motivation to help. A smile of pleasure and a pleasant "thank you" is all that is required. That's what your child wants, just as you want that from your child. Your child is helping in part to reinforce his or her bond with you.

- Realize that your child is growing in very positive ways by helping. The helping is good not just for you, but also for your child. He or she acquires valuable skills and feelings of personal empowerment, self-worth, and belonging by contributing to the family welfare. At the same time, when allowed to help, the child's inborn altruism is nourished, not quashed.

References

Alcala, L., Rogoff, B., Mejia-Arauz, R., Coppens, A. D., & Dexter, A. L. (2014). Children's initiative in contributions to family work in indigenous-heritage and cosmopolitan communities in Mexico. *Human Development*, 57, 96-115.

Deci, E. L., Koestner, R., & Ryan, R. M. (1999). A meta-analytic review of experiments examining the effects of extrinsic rewards on intrinsic motivation. *Psychological Bulletin*, 125, 627–668.

Lancy, D., Bock, J., & Gaskins, S. (2010). *The anthropology of learning in childhood*. Lanham, MD: AltaMire Press.

Lepper, M. R., Greene, D., & Nisbett, R. E. (1973). Undermining children's intrinsic interest with extrinsic reward: A test of the "overjustification" hypothesis. *Journal of Personality and Social Psychology*, 28, 129 –137.

Rheingold, H. (1982). Little children's participation in the work of adults: A nascent prosocial behavior. *Child Development*, 53, 114-125.

Rogoff, B., Mejia-Arauz, R., & Correa-Chavez, M. (2015). A cultural paradigm—learning by observing and pitching in. *Advances in Child Development and Behavior*, 49, 1-22.

Warneken, F., & Tomasello, M. (2008). Extrinsic rewards undermine altruistic tendencies in 20-month-olds. *Developmental Psychology*, 44, 1785-1788.

Warneken, F., & Tomasello, M. (2009). The roots of human altruism. *British Journal of Psychology*, 100, 455-471.

11

Infants' Instincts to Help, Share, and Comfort

*Moral growth is promoted when we allow
little ones to act on their instincts*

SEPTEMBER 30, 2018

An all-too-common belief in our culture—often held implicitly rather than explicitly—is that babies come into the world as either asocial (the "blank slate" belief) or antisocial (the "original sin" belief) and must be deliberately trained through reward, punishment, and coaxing to be helpful to others. However, parents who are truly attuned to their infants and toddlers are often amazed at the degree to which they behave in prosocial ways without any apparent training or even encouragement. [Note: Prosocial is the technical descriptor, opposite of antisocial, that psychologists commonly use to refer to behaviors aimed at benefiting others.]

An ever-growing mound of research supports the view that babies come to us prewired for prosociality. From an evolutionary perspective, this is not surprising. Throughout our biological history as humans, our survival, both as individuals and as groups, has depended on our helping one another. In the course of natural selection, individuals lacking a natural willingness or even eagerness to be helpful would have had great difficulty, over the long run, in being accepted and supported by the group, and, because of that, would have had great difficulty surviving or reproducing.

Researchers who study prosocial behavior in young children commonly categorize it into three relatively distinct but overlapping categories—helping, sharing (or giving), and comforting (Dunfield, 2014). In the previous essay in this series, I presented evidence that little children begin voluntarily helping with housework and other chores almost as soon as they are able to move around, and, if those activities are accepted rather than discouraged, the helping becomes ever more effective as the children grow older. Now I continue the theme of natural prosociality by summarizing some of the research on infants' natural tendencies to share and comfort.

Sharing

Very early in life, infants routinely, without any special encouragement, begin to give objects to their caregivers and even to unfamiliar other adults and children. In a series of experiments conducted in the United States many years ago, every one of 111 infants who was tested, ages 12 to 18 months, spontaneously gave toys to an adult during brief sessions in a laboratory playroom (Hay & Murray, 1982; Rheingold &

others, 1976; also mentioned in Essay 8 of this collection). They gave not just to their mothers or fathers but also to an unfamiliar experimenter, and they gave new toys as frequently as familiar ones. They gave when an adult requested a toy by holding out a hand with palm up (the universal requesting posture), and they gave when no requests were made. Since then, research across cultures suggests that this early, natural tendency to give occurs among young children everywhere. For example, in one study infants in a Ju/'hoansi hunter-gatherer community in Africa were observed to give objects regularly to others before the end of their first year of life (Bakeman & others, 1990). Ju/'hoansi adults celebrate and deliberately nurture this early giving by playing games of back-and-forth giving of objects such as beads with infants (Bakeman & others, 1990). There is good reason to believe that such games increase infants' future tendencies to give.

An experiment in the United States, with infants as young as 7 months, showed that the frequency of giving toys and other objects to an unfamiliar adult (the experimenter) increased after practice with games of give-and-take (Xu, Saether, & Sommerville, 2016). In the experiment, each infant was tested twice in a laboratory playroom, 7 to 14 days apart. The mothers of some of the infants were instructed to play give-and-take games (passing objects back and forth) with their infants during the period between the two tests, and other mothers were instructed to play games of dropping objects into a bucket during that period. The result was a great increase in spontaneous giving, in the second test compared to the first, for those in the give-and-take practice condition but not for those in the control (bucket) condition. Playing the bucket game had no effect on the rate of spontaneous giving nor, even, on the rate of dropping of things into buckets.

Apparently, giving is special not just in the sense that it appears early without training, but also in that it increases dramatically when there is opportunity to practice it and others seem to appreciate it. In this way, giving appears to be like helping, as discussed in the previous essay; it appears naturally very early in the child's development and will persist and increase if it is welcomed by adults in the child's world.

Comforting

Newborn babies, as young as 2 or 3 days old, reflexively cry and show other signs of distress in response to another baby's crying. They show more distress to crying than to other equally loud and discordant sounds, and they even show more distress to recorded sounds of another infant's crying than to recordings of their own crying (see Little et al., 2015). Researchers have suggested that this early natural tendency to feel discomfort in response to another's discomfort is a foundation for the development of empathy and caring.

Researchers have found that, by 8 months of age, infants no longer cry in response to another infants' crying, but, instead, behave in ways that seem to comfort the other infant. Mitzi-Jane Little and her colleagues (2015) conducted an experiment in which 8-month-olds were brought into the laboratory in sets of three and placed in strollers, in a triangular arrangement, such that each of them could see the other two and could, with effort, reach out and touch either of them. In some cases the infants' mothers were present (standing to the side of their infant), and in others the mothers were not present. The goal was to see how the other two infants would respond if any one of the three began to fuss or cry. The result was quite remarkable: In every case, the infants who were not fussing or crying looked directly at the distressed infant and, in many cases, behaved in ways that seemed to be designed to comfort that infant, such as vocalizing (e.g. cooing), waving, and reaching toward and sometimes touching the distressed infant. They did this whether or not their own mothers, who were instructed to remain passive, were present. These comforting responses caused the distressed infant to stop fussing or crying more than one-third of the time that they occurred.

As infants grow older and more mobile, they begin to comfort distressed others in more complex ways, such as by giving objects that they think will be comforting (Hoffman, 2000; Knafo et al., 2008). By about two years old, young children are often quite effective at such comforting. As an example, Martin Hoffman (2000) described a case in which 2-year-old David first attempted to comfort his crying friend by giving him his (David's) own teddy bear. When that didn't work, David ran to the next room and returned with his friend's teddy bear and gave it to him. The friend hugged the bear and immediately stopped crying. To behave in such an effective manner, the child must not only feel bad about another's discomfort but must also understand enough about the other person to know what will provide comfort.

Freedom and Acceptance as Prerequisite Conditions for Moral Development

A major theme emerging from research with young children is that freedom and acceptance are key ingredients to their healthy development. To an amazing degree, children know innately what they must do to develop in healthy ways, but we must permit and welcome those activities, and we must provide an environment that enables them to occur. This applies to physical, intellectual, and emotional development, as I have explained elsewhere (e.g., Gray, 2013), and it also, as explained here and in the previous essay, applies to social/moral development. Life would be easier and more joyful for everyone if more people realized this.

References

Bakeman, R., Adamson, L. B., Konner, M., and Barr, R., (1990). !Kung infancy: The social context of object exploration. *Child Development*, 61, 794-809.

Dunfield, K. (2014). A construct divided: Prosocial behavior as helping, sharing, and comforting subtypes. *Frontiers in Psychology*, 5, 1-13.

Gray, P. (2013). *Free to Learn: Why Unleashing the Instinct to Play Will Make Our Children Happier, More Self-Reliant, and Better Students for Life*. New York: Basic Books, 2013.

Hay, D. F., & Murray, P. (1982). Giving and requesting: Social facilitation of infants' offers to adults. *Infant Behavior and Development*, 5, 301-310.

Hoffman, M. (2000). *Empathy and moral development: Implications for caring and justice*. Cambridge, England: Cambridge University Press.

Knafo, A., Zahn-Waxler, C., Van Hulle, C., Robinson, J. L., & Rhee, S. H (2008). The developmental origins of a disposition toward empathy: Genetic and environmental contributions. *Emotion*, 8, 737-752.

Liddle M.-J. E., Bradley B. S., & McGrath A. (2015). Baby empathy: Infant distress and peer prosocial responses. *Infant Mental Health Journal*, 36, 446-458

Rheingold, H. L., Hay, D. F., & West, M. J (1976). Sharing in the second year of life. *Child Development*, 47, 1148-1158.

Xu, J., Saether, L., & Sommerville, J. (2016). Experience facilitates the emergence of sharing behavior among 7.5-month-old infants. Developmental Psychology, 52, 1732-1743.

12

The Age Four Transition to Responsible Childhood

Converging evidence shows a major shift toward independence around age 4

DECEMBER 29, 2018

My earliest clear memories of events I experienced, which are not simply memories of stories told to me about my childhood, are from when I was 4 years old. I know that I was 4 because those memories are clearly situated at and near the apartment in Minneapolis where we lived when I was 4, from which we moved shortly after I turned 5. One of those memories, which would have occurred when I was about 4 years and 4 months, is the following. On a hot summer day, my grandmother told me that it was time for me to take an adventure by myself. We lived on a busy street with traffic lights, and I'm sure that my grandmother had already explained to me how to cross streets at lights as we took walks together. But this day, she told me, I would go by myself, a distance of about two blocks, crossing at least one busy street, to buy myself a popsicle and then walk back home. She would sit on the stoop and watch to make sure I came back OK. I did. And then after that, I could take walks like that myself, to get things my grandmother or others in the family needed, without having to be watched. I'm sure that one reason I remember this event so well is that it was very exciting to me, a big step toward growing up.

There are a number of significant things to note about this memory. First, this was seven decades ago, back when it wasn't unusual to see little kids walking along the sidewalk and crossing streets unaccompanied by an adult. There was no fear that someone would call the police or Child Protective Services. If Jack were 4 years old, you might not want to trust him to make a good bargain on his sale of the cow (he might trade it for beans), but you could trust him to walk to the marketplace and find his way back. Second, this illustrates something that parents (or grandparents, as in my case) did in those days; they taught kids safety rules, so they could safely gain independence, rather than protecting them from independence. But the point I want to elaborate on now has to do with motivational and cognitive changes that occur in children at around age 4, which make children both desirous of and capable of increased independence. It is significant that back then, it would have been fairly common to see 4-year-olds out on adventures by themselves, but not 3-year-olds. Three-year-olds might be out with their 5-year-old siblings, but rarely if ever alone.

The Age of Independence in Hunter-Gatherer Bands and Sudbury Schools

Some years ago, I delved into the lives of children in hunter-gatherer bands by surveying anthropologists and reading all I could find on the topic. One thing I learned is that hunter-gatherers typically view children as "infants" up until about 4 years old, and as "children who have sense" (to use a phrase quoted by one anthropologist) beginning at about 4 years old (Gray, 2012). Children under age 4 are often still nursed by their mothers, and although they are free to engage in many adventures around the campsite and to accompany adults or older children on trips, they are not allowed to—and apparently have little desire to—venture out of sight and hearing of adult or older-child caregivers. Four-year-olds, in contrast, are generally free to run with the other kids, or even alone, away from caregivers. Millennia of experience have taught hunter-gatherers that by the age of about 4 (of course, it varies somewhat from child to child), children not only begin to seek independence from adults, but are generally capable of it.

When I first became interested in the Sudbury Valley School, well before my research into hunter-gatherers, I was intrigued to learn that the youngest students the school would accept were 4 years old. At this school, all students, regardless of age, are free to roam anywhere on the school's 10-acre campus, which is not fenced off from its surrounds. Adults do not follow the students around. Students, regardless of age, are expected to take responsibility for their own safety. The campus includes a millpond with a dam and is bordered on one side by a road with traffic and on another side by a state forest where a person could get lost. It also has huge rocks and trees to climb and one of those old-fashioned, "dangerous" high slides in the playground. The judgment of the school has always been that most 4-year-olds are capable of being responsible for their own safety in this environment, but most 3-year-olds are not. (I should add that the school requires a visiting week of all prospective students, regardless of age, in which they must prove their ability to be responsible; so not all 4-year-olds are accepted.) The policy has turned out to be wise. Over the school's 50-year history, no students have died or even been seriously injured. The policy has since been adopted by most of the schools throughout the world that are modeled after Sudbury Valley.

The Shift From Attachment to Independence

If you read the literature on child development and advice to parents—especially if you read the older literature, before "experts" began to see it as their job to frighten people—you will find a continuous refrain about how, at age 4, children begin to need and seek greater independence from adults. Even today, some of that can be found in quotes on the Internet if you Google "children age 4." Here are three examples from my cursory search:

"'Children this age [age 4] go from 0 to 60 on the independence scale, so it's vital to talk to them about safety rules before they get any big ideas,' says Daniel Coury, M.D., chief of developmental and behavioral pediatrics at Nationwide

Children's Hospital, in Columbus, Ohio. 'But you don't want to scare them off.'"

"Four-year-olds want to try new experiences. They also want to be more self-reliant and seek to expand the areas of their lives where they can be independent decision-makers."

"What a four-year-old would say about his or her needs: 'I need to explore, to try out, and to test limits.'"

Research on attachment, going all the way back to the classic work of John Bowlby (1958) and Mary Ainsworth (1979), has revealed that children's attachment to caregivers begins to increase around age 6 to 8 months and begins to decline at about age 4 years. From an evolutionary perspective, this makes perfect sense. Six to 8 months is when infants begin to move around on their own (initially by crawling), so a strong drive to be near a reliable caregiver promotes their survival by reducing the chance that they will stray off too far and get into danger. At around 4 years children begin to have common sense, so there is much reduced danger in their straying off. The primary function of attachment is to protect children from danger during the period when they are mobile but have not yet acquired much sense about what is dangerous and what isn't.

The Internalization of Language and Origin of Verbal Thought

What underlies the increased ability of children, at about age 4, to behave safely and independently? Part of the answer, of course, simply has to do with increased knowledge. If caregivers have done their job properly and allowed children to explore and behave in moderately risky ways in the caregivers' presence during the children's first four years, then, by about age 4, children have learned a lot about what is safe and what isn't. But something less gradual also occurs just before or around age 4: Children develop the capacity to use words not just to communicate with others, but also to communicate with themselves. In other words, they begin to think verbally, which means that they can tell themselves what is safe or not and can recall verbal rules that they learned from others, and they can use those abilities to restrain or motivate their actions as they roam and explore on their own.

The person most noted for this theory that a major shift in thinking occurs around age 4 is the Russian developmental psychologist Lev Vygotsky (1934/1962). Vygotsky contended that what we usually describe as thinking is, largely, internalized speech. At first, according to Vygotsky, thinking occurs in a social context, as back-and-forth speech with others. An older person says something to the child. The child understands what was said and may or may not argue. If the statement is a rule of behavior, the child may abide by it immediately, but not sometime later, because the child doesn't think of it later. That's why very young children need to be watched. Over time, however, children learn that they can use language even when not in the presence of others, as a way of reminding themselves what they should or should not do. At first, they may use the words aloud, in a phase of talking to themselves: "Oh, Mommy said don't touch the hot stove." But with time, they learn that they don't have to actually enunciate the words; they can just think them to themselves. There is sometimes a transitional period where you can see the child's lips move as he or she thinks. If you are a lip reader, you can literally read the child's mind.

According to Vygotsky, and verified by much research since his time, by about age 4, children have developed the capacity for verbal thought to such a degree that they can recall and follow rules that they learned previously without someone there to remind them, and can even think verbally about how to behave in new contexts (Alderson-Day & Fernyhough, 2015; Manfra et al., 2014; Winsler et al., 1997). They can ask themselves questions such as, "Is it safe for me to do this?" or "What would happen if I did that?" and imagine the answer before they actually try this or that. This ability is the essence of common sense and caution.

The Emerging Understanding of Minds

Another well-documented cognitive shift that occurs at around age 4 concerns what researchers call "theory of mind" (e.g., Wellman, Cross, & Watson, 2001). Theory of mind refers to the understanding that there is a difference between what a person may believe to be true and what is actually true. People can hold, and act upon, false beliefs. One person can believe one thing, and another can believe something else. This understanding is a crucial development in the child's ability to get along with peers. To have real friends and to truly collaborate, you must understand that the thoughts and perspectives of the friend are not necessarily the same as yours. It is no co-incidence, I think, that this ability emerges around the same time that children are motivated and able to enjoy play with age-mates, without intervention by adults or older children. Most 4-year-olds, unlike most 3-year-olds, can play happily and socially with others their own age, because they can take into account the needs and knowledge of their playmates, which may be different from their own needs and knowledge.

I suspect (though I don't know of any research on it) that the development of theory of mind is intimately linked to the internalization of language. When children talk to themselves as a way of thinking, they almost can't help but begin to become aware of the fact that they have a mind, and that their mind can change over time: "I think there is a toy in this box. Now I'm opening the box. Oops, there's no toy. I was wrong." Once they realize that they have a mind, which can change over time in its knowledge and beliefs, it is a relatively small step to realize that the same is true for other people. The mind is what people say to themselves.

It is also no coincidence, then, that age 4 is when children typically begin to enjoy tricks and riddles and guessing games. To enjoy these things, you have to understand that the mind can be fooled. Understanding this also helps you to behave safely when out adventuring. You know that your current belief, or what a playmate just told you, could be wrong, so you test it before you act on it.

Conclusion

Throughout human history, until very recently, people understood that the capacity for common sense, restraint, and self-controlled safety grows rather rapidly at around age 4. Age 4 was understood as the approximate age at which children become focused on peers and begin to learn at least as much, if not more, from play with peers as from interactions with adults. People didn't need research studies to prove it to them; it was obvious. Children today, sadly, exist in a world in which adults have become convinced that children are not competent at age 4, and many believe that they are not competent even at age 8 or 12. Many 12-year-olds today are not permitted the independence that 4-year-olds were permitted until just a few decades ago.

We also, sadly, live at a time when many people hold the really weird belief that it is more important to train little children in so-called "academic skills" than to teach them basic rules of safety—rules that they can understand and could give them the freedom they need to learn lessons that are far more important than the scraps of academia we force onto them before they are ready.

References

Ainsworth, M. (1979). Attachment as related to mother-infant interaction. *Advances in the Study of Behavior*, 9, 2-52.

Alderson-Day, B., & Fernyhough, C. (2015). Inner speech: Development, cognitive functions, phenomenology, and neurobiology. *Psychological Bulletin*, 141, 931–965.

Bowlby, J. (1958). The nature of the child's tie to his mother. *International Journal of Psychoanalysis*, 39, 350-373.

Gray, P. (2012). The value of a play-filled childhood in development of the hunter-gatherer individual. In Narvaez, D., Panksepp, J., Schore, A., & Gleason, T. (Eds.), *Evolution, early experience and human development: From research to practice and policy*, pp 252-370. New York: Oxford University Press

Manfra, L., Davis, K., Ducenne, L., & Winsler, A. (2014). Preschoolers' motor and verbal self-control strategies during a resistance-to-temptation task. *Journal of Genetic Psychology: Research and Theory on Human Development*, 175, 332-345.

Vygotsky, L. (1934, English translation, 1962). *Thought and Language*. Cambridge, MA: MIT Press.

Wellman, H. M., Cross, D., & Watson, J. (2001). Meta-analysis of theory-of-mind development: The truth about false-belief. *Child Development*, 72, 655-684.

Winsler, A., Diaz, R., & de Madrid, I. (1997). The role of private speech in the transition from collaborative to independent task performance in young children. *Early Childhood Research Quarterly*, 12, 59-79.

13

How Can Children Learn Bravery
in an Age of Overprotection?

*It is dangerous to try to protect
children from all dangers*

DECEMBER 8, 2011

In the spring of 2008, Lenore Skenazy, a resident of Queens
in New York City, left her 9-year-old son at Bloomingdale's in
midtown Manhattan, in the middle of a sunny Sunday, gave
him a handful of quarters, $20 for emergencies, a map and a
Metrocard, and said he could go home himself. To do so he
would have to take the subway and a bus, on a route he had
taken many times before with his mom. When he arrived at
home he was pleased as punch. He had been begging for this
opportunity to prove that he could get home himself by public
transportation, and now he had done it. He glowed with his
new sense of maturity.

Lenore, who was then a columnist for the *New York Sun*,
wrote a column about it. Within hours after the column

appeared, some in the media had labeled her as "America's Worst Mom". In a rare show of unity, all of the women on ABC's *The View* soundly condemned her decision. According to Lenore, the more polite of the other fourth-grade moms at the playground she and her son frequented said things like, "Well, that's fine, and I'll let my son do that too . . . when he's in college." Lenore used this incident as a trigger to write a wonderfully humorous yet serious book entitled *Free Range Kids*, in which she counters parental and societal fears by showing how unreasonable so many of them are.

Now, I don't mean to one-up Lenore—whom I admire greatly and with whom I now collaborate—in the America's worst parent department, BUT . . . My son, at age 13, went to London for two weeks by himself. That was back in 1982, when it was more acceptable to be a trustful parent than in 2008 or today. He had approached his mom and me in the spring, when he was still 12, with his request to take that trip. He would earn all the money for the trip himself, so we couldn't use money as an excuse to stop him. He would plan the whole trip himself—in fact, he had already planned much of it. He wanted to prove to himself that he could organize and do something this complicated without adult help. He also wanted to see certain castles and museum treasures, which he had been reading about and were prominent in the Dungeons and Dragons games he played. He had never been abroad. Neither, for that matter, had his mom or I at that point in our lives.

We hesitated about saying yes. "Not because of your age," we explained, "but because of your diabetes." He had (and, of course, still has) Type 1 diabetes. He had been testing his own sugar levels, giving himself insulin injections, and regulating his diet appropriately ever since his diabetes first appeared, at age 9. He was as good at all of this as any adult diabetic I knew. Yet, it is dangerous for anyone with insulin-dependent diabetes to travel alone. There's always the risk of insulin-induced hypoglycemia, in which you lose judgment and even consciousness. What if that happened while he was away, in a strange place, and nobody helped him?

To all this, he said, in essence: "I'll always have diabetes. If you're telling me that I can't travel alone because of diabetes, you're telling me that I'll never be able to travel alone. I don't accept that. I'm not going to let diabetes prevent me from doing what I want to do. When I'm older I'll travel alone and you won't be able to stop me. If it's not age you're concerned about, then what's the difference between my traveling now and my traveling when I'm 18, or 30, or 50?" His logic, as always, was impeccable.

We said, "OK." We fulfilled our parental obligation to nag only by asking him to promise to wear his MedicAlert medallion everywhere, so if he did have an insulin reaction people could read it and see that he was diabetic and needed help and would not assume that he was drunk. We didn't need to nag; he would have worn that anyway.

He spent the rest of that spring and all summer working and earning all the money he needed for the trip. He earned most of it through a job at a small restaurant, which he got on his own. At first he washed dishes, but then, when they saw what a good worker he was, they promoted him to working the grill and coordinating the kitchen. That in itself was a wonderful growth experience. By October, he was ready to take his adventure. He was by then 13 years old. He was a student at Sudbury Valley School, with its broad view of education, so taking time off from school was no problem. Everyone at the school understood that this trip was a valuable educational experience, so for the duration of the trip they marked him as in attendance but on a field trip.

He was abroad and out of touch with us for two weeks, saw countless castles, toured Westminster, spent days immersed in the treasures of the National Gallery and other museums, and took walking tours all over London. He also took a side trip to Oxford for a Moody Blues concert, another to Cardiff to walk the hills and see Cardiff Castle, and another to Paris with a 15-year-old young lady he had met on the airplane to London and who was also traveling alone. All in all, it was an amazing set of experiences that led him to new heights in confidence about his ability to run his own life. Diabetes diashmetes.

Now, I'll be the first to admit that my son was not just any 13-year-old kid when he took this adventure. Had he been less responsible and less able to think things through, his mother and I might have said no. To be a trustful parent is not to be a negligent parent. You have to know your child. But responsibility does not grow in a vacuum. If you want responsible kids, you have to allow them the freedom to be responsible, and that, sadly, is much harder to do today than it was in 1982; and in 1982 it was harder than in years before that.

Today it would be almost impossible for parents to let their child have an adventure like the one that my son had at the age of 13, no matter how responsible the child might be. For starters, that job of working the grill at a restaurant, where he earned the money for the trip, is now illegal for anyone under 16 years old (in our home state of Massachusetts). The state itself has decided that children under 16, just by virtue of their age, are incompetent and irresponsible. And, on the matter of social pressure, even in 1982 our decision raised a few eyebrows. Imagine how your friends and relatives would react if you, as a parent today, made such a decision.

But, at other times and places people might have wondered more about our hesitation than about our final decision. As Lenore says in the introduction to her book, "[Our great, great grandparents] sent their sweet children out on slow, rusty steamers to the New World with only a couple of rubles and a hard salami."

To illustrate the enormous contrast between our own infantilizing of children and the view of people in traditional cultures, here is a quotation from Mary Martini (1994), about her observations of little children on the Marquesan island of 'Ua Pou, in the South Pacific:

"Thirteen members of a stable play group were observed daily for four months and less systematically for another two . . .. Children ranged from two to five years old. They played several hours a day without supervision while their siblings attended school nearby. They organized activities, settled disputes, avoided danger, dealt with injuries, distributed goods, and negotiated contact with passing others—without adult intervention. They avoided adults, probably because adults disrupted their play. The play area was potentially dangerous. A strong surf broke on the boat ramp. The large rocks on the shore were strewn with broken glass. The valley walls were steep and slippery. Children played on a high bridge and high, sharp, lava rock walls. Machetes, axes, and matches were occasionally left around and young children played with these. In spite of these dangers, accidents were rare and minor. Hitting, teasing, and scolding were frequent, but fistfights, tantrums, and prolonged crying were rare. Disputes were frequent but were dissipated after a few minutes. Children did not seek adults or older children to settle conflicts or direct their play."

Martini goes on to explain that, in this group, the 4- and 5-year-olds cared for the 2- and 3-year-olds, and they did so almost entirely in the context of their play. She found that 24% of their time was involved in sociodramatic (shared fantasy) play, generally at themes relevant to the adult culture, such as "ship," "fishing," "hunting," and "preparing for feasts". Another 30% was spent at object play (building things), and 28% was spent at physical play (chasing games, climbing, and so on). All this without any adult supervision.

When Martini asked parents about their children's playing with matches and machetes, she found that they would take those things away when they knew about it, because they were afraid that the children would waste the matches and ruin the machetes, not because they were afraid that the children would hurt themselves. According to Martini, the children on this island were remarkably well adjusted psychologically and socially. They didn't whine or demand adult attention as Western children often do, and they were extraordinarily adept at solving their own problems as they arose.

I doubt if there has ever been any human culture, anywhere, at any time, that underestimates children's abilities more than we North Americans do today. Our underestimation becomes a self-fulfilling prophesy, because, by depriving children of freedom, we deprive them of the opportunities they need to learn how to take control of their own behavior and emotions.

Nothing in life is without risk. When we deprive our children of taking the risks that they must take to grow in competence, confidence, and courage, we run the greater and ultimately more tragic risk that they will never learn to take charge of their own lives. So, be brave and let your children be brave.

References

Mary Martini, M. (1994). Peer interactions in Polynesia: A view from the Marquesas. In J. L. Roopnarine, J. E. Johnson, & F. H. Hooper (Eds.), *Children's play in diverse cultures* (pp. 73-103). State University of New York Press.

Skenazy, L. (2009). *Free-range kids: Giving our children the freedom we had without going nuts with worry.* Jossy-Bass.

14

The Culture of Childhood

We've Almost Destroyed It

*Children learn the most valuable lessons
with other children, away from adults*

OCTOBER 31, 2016

I don't want to trivialize the roles of adults in children's lives, but truth be told, we adults greatly exaggerate our roles in our theories and beliefs about how children develop. We have an adult-centric view that we raise, socialize, and educate children.

Certainly, we are important in children's lives. Children need us. We feed, clothe, shelter, and comfort them. We provide examples (not always good) of what it is like to be an adult. But we don't raise, socialize, or educate them. They do all that for themselves, and in that process they more often look to other children than to adults as models. If child psychologists were actually CHILD psychologists (i.e. children themselves), theories of child development would be much less about parents and much more about peers.

Children are biologically designed to grow up in a culture of childhood.

Have you ever noticed how your child's tastes in clothes, music, manner of speech, hobbies, and almost everything else have much more to do with what other children she or he knows are doing or like than what you are doing or like? Children are biologically designed to pay attention to the other children in their lives, to try to fit in with them, to be able to do what they do, to know what they know. Through most of human history, that's how children became educated, and that's still largely how children become educated today, despite our misguided attempts to stop it and turn the educating job over to adults.

Wherever anthropologists have observed traditional cultures and paid attention to children as well as adults, they've observed two cultures: the adults' culture and the children's culture. The two cultures, of course, are not completely independent of one another. They interact and influence one another; and children, as they grow up, gradually leave the culture of childhood and enter into the culture of adulthood. Children's cultures can be understood, at least to some degree, as practice cultures, where children try out various ways of being and practice, modify, and build upon the skills and values of the adult culture.

I first began to think seriously about cultures of childhood when I began looking into band hunter-gatherer societies. In my reading, and in my survey of anthropologists who had lived in such societies, I learned that the children in those societies—from roughly the age of 4 on through their mid-teen years—spent most of their waking time playing and exploring with groups of other children, away from adults (Gray, 2012). They played in age-mixed groups, in which younger children emulated and learned from older ones. I also found that anthropologists who had studied children in other types of traditional cultures also wrote about children's involvement in peer groups as the primary means of their socialization and education (e.g., Lancy et al., 2010; Eibl-Eibesfeldt, 1989). Judith Harris (1998), in a discussion of such research, noted that the popular phrase It takes a village to raise a child is true if interpreted differently from the usual Western interpretation. In her words (p 161): "The reason it takes a village is not because it requires a quorum of adults to nudge erring youngsters back onto the paths of righteousness. It takes a village because in a village there are always enough kids to form a play group."

My own childhood, in Minnesota and Wisconsin in the 1950s, was quite similar to that of children in traditional societies. We had school (which was not the big deal it is today) and chores, and some of us had part time jobs, but most of our waking time was spent with other children away from adults. My family moved frequently, and in each village or city neighborhood to which we moved I found a somewhat different childhood culture, with different games, different traditions, somewhat different values, and different ways of making friends. Whenever we moved, my first big task was to figure out the culture of my new set of peers, so I could become part of it. I was by nature shy, which I think was an advantage because I didn't just blunder in and make a fool of myself. I observed, studied, practiced the skills that I saw were important to my new peers, and then began cautiously to enter in and make friends. Through the early and middle parts of the 20th century, cultures of childhood were found—and in some cases studied by researchers (e.g., Opie & Opie, 1969)—throughout Europe and the United States.

Children learn the most important lessons in life from other children, not from adults.

Why, in the course of natural selection, did children evolve such a strong inclination to spend as much time as possible with other children and avoid adults? With a little reflection, it's not hard to see the reasons. There are many valuable lessons that children can learn in interactions with other children that they cannot learn, or are much less likely to learn, in interactions with adults. Here are some of them.

Authentic Communication

I don't know if this is or is not true in traditional cultures, but in modern Western cultures adults are often terribly condescending toward children. Their communications with children, especially the well-intended ones, are frequently dishonest. Consider, for example, the adult who asks a 4-year old, "What color is that?" while pointing to a red toy fire engine. This is not an honest question. Unless the adult is blind, or color blind, the adult knows perfectly well what color it is. A child would never ask such a stupid question. Almost all the questions that teachers ask, through all the grades of school, are dishonest; the teacher knows the answer (or thinks she does because she read it in the teacher's edition of the textbook), so her question is not really a question; it's a test.

Or consider the adult who says, "Oh, that's beautiful, what a wonderful artist you are," while looking at the child's latest scribbling. Children never give such false praise to one another. Even as children grow older, adults tend to engage them in ways that suggest that either the adults or the children are fools, and often their comments have more to do with trying to teach the children something, or control them in some way, than with genuine attempts to share ideas or really understand the child's ideas.

Little children communicate with one another largely in the context of play, and the communications have real meaning. They negotiate about what and how to play. They discuss the rules. They negotiate in ways very similar to the ways adults negotiate with one another. This is far better practice for future adult-adult communication than the kinds of "conversations" that children typically have with adults. The one research study I have been able to find comparing children's language in different contexts revealed that preschoolers used far more complex language in their fantasy play with other children than in teacher led activities or when they were sitting around a table eating (Fekonja, Marjanovic Umek, & Kranjc, 2005).

As children get older, and especially once they are in their teen years, their communications with one another have ever more to do with the emotions and struggles they experience. They can be honest with their friends, because their friends are not going to overreact and try to assume control, the way that their parents or other adults might. They want to talk about the issues important in their life, but they don't want someone to use those issues as another excuse to subordinate them. They can, with good reason, trust their friends in ways that they cannot trust their parents or teachers.

Independence and Courage

The ultimate goal of childhood is to move away from dependence on parents and establish oneself as one's own person. Already by the age of 2—the "terrible twos," when children's favorite word is "no"—children are clearly on this path. Typically by the age of 4 or a little later, children want to get away from parents and other adults and spend time with other children, where they can try out ways of being that they couldn't try in the presence of adults.

Children's cultures frequently set themselves up as if in opposition to the adults' culture, often quite deliberately and adaptively so. Even young children begin to use scatological, "naughty" words, deliberately flouting adults' dictates. They delight in mocking adults and in finding ways to violate rules. For example, when schools make rules about carrying even toy weapons into school, children bring tiny toy guns and plastic knives to school in their pockets and surreptitiously exhibit them to one another, proudly showing how they violated a seemingly senseless adult-imposed rule (Corsaso & Eder, 1990).

The anthropologist Collin Turbull (1982) noted that children in the hunter-gatherer group he studied would build their own play huts, well away from the main encampment, and would spend some of their time there mocking the adults by exaggerating their blunders and poorly constructed arguments. To learn adaptively from adults, children must not just absorb the good that they see but must also judge and digest the bad, and they can't freely do that when adults are present.

Part of gaining independence is gaining courage—courage to face the challenges and deal with the emergencies that are part of every life. In their play groups, away from adults, children everywhere play in ways that adults might see as dangerous and may want to prevent. They play with sharp knives and fire; they climb trees and dare one another to go higher. Little children, in fantasy play, imagine themselves dealing with trolls, witches, dragons, wolves, and other kinds of predators and murderers. In all such play, children are learning how to manage fear, a crucial skill for anyone who intends to stay alive and well in the face of the real dangers that confront everyone at some points in their lives (Gray, 2019).

In play amongst themselves, children create their own activities and solve their own problems rather than rely on a powerful authority figure to do these for them. This is one of the great values of playing away from adults. In such play they have to, as it were, be the adults, precisely because there are no adults present. Play is the practice space for adulthood. Adults spoil this large purpose of play when they intervene and try to be helpful.

Creating Rules and Understanding their Purpose and Modifiability

A fundamental difference between adults' and children's games is that adults generally abide by fixed, pre-established rules, whereas children generally see rules as modifiable. When adults play baseball, or Scrabble, or almost anything, they generally follow or try to follow the "official" rules of the game. In contrast, when children play they commonly make up the rules as they go along (Youniss, 1994). This is true even when they play games like baseball or Scrabble, if there is no adult present to enforce the official rules. (For my story of how I learned this lesson, about how children play Scrabble, see Gray, 2014). This is one of the ways in which children's play is usually more creative than adults' play.

The famous developmental psychologist Jean Piaget (1932) noted long ago that children develop a more sophisticated and useful understanding of rules when they play with other children than when they play with adults. With adults, they get the impression that rules are fixed, that they come down from some high authority and cannot be changed. But when children play with other children, because of the more equal nature of the relationship, they feel free to challenge one another's ideas about the rules, which often leads to negotiation and change in rules. They learn that most rules are not irreversible mandates but are human contrivances to make life more fun and fair. This is an important lesson; it is a cornerstone of democracy.

Practicing and Building on the Skills and Values of the Adult Culture

Even while differentiating themselves from adult culture, children import features of that culture into theirs. They incorporate into their play many of the skills and values that they observe among adults. This is why children in hunter-gather cultures play at hunting and gathering; why children in farming cultures play at farming; and why children in our culture play at computers. It is also why hunter-gatherer children do not play competitive games (the adults in their culture eschew competition), while children in our culture do play competitive games (though not to the degree that they do when adults are involved).

Children don't just mimic, in play, what they observe among adults. Rather, they interpret what they observe, try out variations, and in that way strive to make sense of adult culture. Children's play is always creative, and in their play they experiment with new, creative variations of themes derived from adults. This is how each new generation builds upon, rather than simply replicates, the culture of their parents' generation.

Children are naturally drawn to the newest innovations in the larger culture around them. Adults are often suspicious of such changes, but children embrace them. This is illustrated today by children's eagerness to learn how to use the latest computer technology; they are often far ahead of their parents in this realm. Children's culture focuses, quite naturally and adaptively, on the skills important to the world they are growing into, not the world as it was when their parents were growing up. Adults in every generation seem to bemoan the fact that their children don't play the way they played when they were kids. That's one more of the reasons why children have to get away from adults to play most adaptively.

Getting Along with Others as Equals

The main difference between adults and children that affects their interaction has to do with power. Adults, because of their greater size, strength, status, experience in the world, and control of resources, have power over children. So, children's interactions with adults are generally unbalanced by a gap in power. If children are going to grow up to be effective adults, they must learn to get along with others as equals. For the most part, they can only practice that with other children, not with adults.

Perhaps the most important function of the culture of childhood is to teach children how to get along with peers. Children practice this constantly in social play. To play with another person, you must pay attention to the other person's needs, not just your own, or the other person will quit.

You must overcome narcissism. You must learn to share. You must learn to negotiate in ways that respect the other person's ideas, not just your own. You must learn how to assert your needs and desires while at the same time understanding and trying to meet the needs and desires of your play-mate. This may be the most important of all skills that human beings must learn for a successful life. Without this ability it is not possible to have a happy marriage, true friends, or co-operative work partners.

The need to learn how to deal with others on an equal power footing is the primary reason why children need to grow up in a culture of childhood. It underlies all of the rest of what children learn best with peers. The reason why children's communications with other children are more authentic than those with adults, why they can practice independence and courage with other children better than with adults, why they can learn about the modifiability of rules with other children better than with adults, and why they can more freely prac-tice adult skills with other children than they can with adults, is that their relationships with other children are relation-ships of equality rather than relationships of dominance and subordinance.

The adult battle against cultures of childhood has been going on for centuries.

Hunter-gatherer adults seemed to understand that children need to grow up largely in a culture of childhood, with little adult interference, but such understanding declined with the rise of agriculture, land ownership, and hierarchical organi-zations of power among adults (Gray, 2012). Adults began to see it as their duty to suppress children's natural willfulness, so as to promote obedience, which often involved attempts to remove them from the influences of other children and subordinate them to adult authority. The first systems of compulsory schooling, which are the forerunners of our schools today, arose quite explicitly for that purpose.

If there is a father of modern schools, it is the Pietist clergyman August Hermann Francke, who developed a system of compulsory schooling in Prussia in the late 17th century, which was subsequently copied and elaborated upon throughout Europe and America. In his instructions to schoolmasters, Francke wrote: "Above all it is necessary to break the natural willfulness of the child. While the schoolmaster who seeks to make the child more learned is to be commended for cultivating the child's intellect, he has not done enough. He has forgotten his most important task, namely that of making the will obedient." Francke believed that the most effective way to break children's wills was through constant monitoring and supervision. He wrote: "Youth do not know how to regulate their lives and are naturally inclined toward idle and sinful behavior when left to their own devices. For this reason, it is a rule in this institution [the Prussian Pietist schools] that a pupil never be allowed out of the presence of a supervisor. The supervisor's presence will stifle the pupil's inclination to sinful behavior, and slowly weaken his willfulness." (The Francke quotations come from Melton, 1988.)

We may today reject Francke's way of stating it, but the underlying premise of much adult policy toward children is still in Francke's tradition. In fact, social forces have conspired now to put Francke's recommendation into practice far more effectively than occurred at Francke's time or any other time in the past. Parents have become convinced that it is dangerous and irresponsible to allow children to play with other children, away from adults, so restrictions on such play are more severe and effective than they have ever been before. By increasing the amount of time spent in school, expanding homework, harping on the importance of scoring high on school tests, banning children from public spaces unless accompanied by an adult, and replacing free play with adult-led sports and lessons, we have created a world in which children are almost always in the presence of a supervisor, who is ready to intervene, protect, and prevent them from practicing courage, independence, and all the rest that children practice best with peers, away from adults. I have argued elsewhere (Gray, 2011, 2013) that this is why we see record levels of anxiety, depression, suicide, and feelings of powerlessness among adolescents and young adults today.

The internet is the savior of children's culture today.

There is, however, one saving grace, one reason why we adults have not completely crushed the culture of childhood. That is the Internet. We've created a world in which children are more or less prevented from congregating in physical space without an adult, but children have found another way. They get together in cyberspace. They play games and communicate over the Internet. They create their own rules and culture and ways of being with others over the Internet. They mock adults and flout adult rules over the Internet. They, especially teenagers, share thoughts and feelings with friends through texting and social media, and they stay several steps ahead of their parents and other adults in finding new ways to maintain their privacy in all of this (for a large-scale study documenting this, see boyd, 2014). That's not enough. They need to be able to get together without adults in physical space, too. But it's better than nothing.

Of course, the hew and cry we keep hearing from so many educators and parenting "experts" now is that we must ban or limit children's "screen time". Yes, if we all did that, while still banning them from public spaces without adult supervision, we would finally succeed in crushing the culture of childhood. We would prevent children from educating themselves in the ways that they always have, and we would see the rise of a generation of adults who don't know how to be adults because they never had a chance to practice it.

References

boyd, d. (2014). *It's complicated: The social lives of networked teens.* Yale University Press.

Corsaro, W. A., & Eder, D. (1990). Children's peer cultures. Annual Reviews of Sociology, 16, 197-200.

Eibl-Eibesfeldt, I. (1989). *Human ethology.* Hawthorne, NY: Aldine de Gruyter.

Fekonja, U., Marjanovic Umek, L., & Kranjc, S. (2005). Free play and other daily preschool activities as a context for child's language development. *Studia Psychologica*, 47, 103-116.

Gray, P. (2011). The decline of play and the rise of psychopathology in childhood and adolescence. *American Journal of Play*, 3, 443-463. 2011.

Gray, P. (2012). The value of a play-filled childhood in development of the hunter-gatherer individual. In Narvaez, D., Panksepp, J., Schore, A., & Gleason, T. (Eds.), *Evolution, early experience and human development: From research to practice and policy.* New York: Oxford University Press, 2012.

Gray, P. (2013). *Free to learn: Why unleashing the instinct to play will make our children happier, more self-reliant, and better students for life.* Basic Books.

Gray, P. (2014). A playful path, and DeKoven's advice for getting back on it. *Psychology Today*, March 13, 2014. Available at https://www.psychologytoday.com/us/blog/freedom-learn/201403/
playful-path-and-dekovens-advice-getting-back-it

Gray, P. (2020). Risky play: Why children love and need it. In Loebach, J., Little, S., Cox, A., & Owens, P. E. (Eds.), *Fostering the inclusion of youth in the public realm: Design processes, practices, and policies for the creation of youth-inclusive public outdoor environments.* Routledge. (In press for 2020 publication.)

Harris, J. R. (1998). *The nurture assumption: Why children turn out the way they do.* New York: Free Press.

Lancy, D. F., Bock, J., & Gaskins, S. (2010). The anthropology of learning in childhood. Lanham, MD: AltaMira Press.

Melton, J. V. H. (1988). *Absolutism and the eighteenth-century origins of compulsory schooling in Prussia and Austria.* Cambridge: Cambridge University Press.

Opie, I., & Opie, P. (1984). *Children's games in street and playground.* Oxford, UK: Oxford University Press.

Piaget, J. (1932, 1965). *The moral judgment of the child.* New York: Free Press.

Turnbull, C. M. (1982). The ritualization of potential conflict between the sexes among the Mbuti. In E. G. Leacock & R. B. Lee (Eds.), *Politics and history in band societies*, 133-155. Cambridge: Cambridge University Press.

Youniss, J. (1994). Children's friendships and peer culture: Implications for theories of networks and support. In F. Nestmann & K. Hurrelmann (Eds.), *Social networks and social support in childhood and adolescence*. Berlin, Germany: Walter de Gruyter.

15

The ADHD Personality

A Normal and Valuable Human Variation

*For good evolutionary reasons, some
people are highly impulsive.*

AUGUST 19, 2010

Last month I posted an essay linking the dramatic increase
in diagnosed ADHD (Attention Deficit Hyperactivity Disorder) to our increasingly restrictive system of schooling (Gray,
2010). I presented evidence there that (a) the official, DSM-
IV diagnostic criteria for ADHD focus primarily on school-
related issues such as sitting in seat, completing assignments,
and not interrupting teachers; (b) most diagnoses of ADHD
begin with referrals from teachers or other school personnel;
(c) teachers' ratings, if used alone, would produce far more
ADHD diagnoses than is the case when those ratings are bal-
anced by parents' ratings; and (d) the rapid increase in ADHD
diagnoses occurred over the same period that high-stakes

standardized testing increasingly dominated the school environment.

My overriding point was that, because of the increased competitive and standardized nature of schooling, behaviors that in the past would have been regarded as within the range of normal are now considered to be abnormal. At present, in the United States, roughly 12% of boys and 4% of girls have been diagnosed with ADHD. What kind of a society are we if we consider 12% of boys (one out of every eight) to be mentally disordered in this way and in need of strong psychoactive drugs as treatment? [Note added in June, 2015. Now things are worse than when I wrote this post. According to the most recent data, 20% of school-aged boys have been diagnosed with ADHD.]

Some people who commented on that post objected to my sociological analysis by referring to evidence that the brains of people diagnosed with ADHD are in some ways different from those of other people. To them, the evidence of a brain difference is somehow proof that ADHD is a "medical" or "biological" disorder and that a sociological analysis of it is out of place. But if you give it some thought, you will quickly realize that there is no contradiction at all between biological and sociological analyses of ADHD or any other condition referred to as a disorder. My goal in that essay was to explain the extraordinary increase in rate of ADHD diagnosis that has occurred over the last two or three decades. I don't think that increase is primarily due to a change in brain structures in the general population; I think it is primarily due to a change in social values and especially in the conditions of schooling.

Today, as a society, we are far less tolerant of children who don't adapt well to our system of compulsory schooling than we were in the past, and so we diagnose them and give them drugs.

For a somewhat (but not fully) analogous case, consider homosexuality. Homosexuality is biologically a condition of the brain; but the decision to label it as a disorder, or not a disorder, is a social judgment. Until 1973, homosexuality was on the American Psychiatric Association's list of official mental disorders, but in that year it was removed. Suddenly, gay people were no longer "disordered." That decision clearly reflected a change in social values, a change that made it possible for people with the brain condition of homosexuality to live happier lives than they had been able to before, when they more or less had to stay in the closet and were subject to terrible abuse and even arrest if they did not. With regard to homosexuality we have as a society become more liberal and accepting. With regard to the kind of childhood rambunctiousness and impulsiveness that leads to a diagnosis of ADHD, however, we have as a society become less liberal and accepting.

The story for ADHD, of course, is not fully analogous to that for homosexuality. The condition we call ADHD is clearly one that can vary in degree. A few people—and I think that is very few people—who are diagnosed with ADHD have the condition to such an extreme degree that most of us would consider it to be a disorder, worthy of some kind of treatment, under almost any social conditions. But most people with the diagnosis have the condition to a much lesser degree than that—a degree that interferes especially with schooling and certain other school-like activities, as they are structured today, but may actually be helpful in other settings.

In the remainder of this essay I'll summarize current thinking concerning the cognitive and neural foundations for ADHD and explain further why I think our focus should be on changing our system of schooling to accommodate children's diversity rather than on changing children's brain physiology to accommodate schooling.

ADHD Characterized as High Impulsiveness and Reduced "Executive Control"

According to the most widely accepted cognitive model of it, the fundamental problem in ADHD is not one of attention so much as one of impulsiveness (initially proposed by Barkley et al., 1997). By a wide variety of measures, people diagnosed with ADHD are more impulsive, less reflective and controlled, than other people. This impulsiveness is believed to underlie all or most of the distinguishing behavioral characteristics shown by such people. Impulsiveness leads them to be easily distractible, which is why they are seen as inattentive. It also leads them to be impatient and restless, unable to tolerate tedium or to sit still unless something truly grabs and retains their interest, which is why they may be seen as hyperactive. And it leads them to be highly emotionally reactive; they tend to respond immediately, emotionally, overtly, to stressful or otherwise arousing situations. The model is no doubt overly simplistic, but it is nevertheless useful as a beginning point for thinking and talking about ADHD.

Cognitive psychologists and neuroscientists commonly use the term executive control to label the mechanisms by which the brain inhibits impulsive behavior, reflects, and then acts on the basis of reflection rather than impulse. Although executive control is generally thought of as a good thing, it seems obvious that it can also, if too strong, be harmful. The opposite of impulsive is inhibited. Some people are too inhibited for their own good. They stew constantly over what is the right thing to do, or over the possible negative consequences of every alternative, and therefore they don't do anything. While the highly controlled person sits and watches an emergency, trying to figure out the best possible response and worrying about the risks, the impulsive person jumps in and saves someone's life.

The Value of Human Diversity in Degree of Impulsiveness Versus Control

Most psychologists would say that psychological wellbeing is maximized by a certain optimal degree of executive control. The overly controlled person suffers from too much inhibition, and the overly impulsive person suffers from too little of it. I agree with that when we are talking about extremes. However, between the extremes there is a broad range on the control-impulsiveness dimension that is potentially quite compatible with psychological wellbeing and contribution to society. The trick, for each person, is to find niches within their environment that play to their strengths rather than to their weaknesses. In general, people who are highly controlled are great in jobs that require lots of reflection and relatively little action, and people who are highly impulsive are great in jobs that require lots of action with relatively little time for reflection. This has nothing to do with degree of intelligence. You can be intelligent and impulsive, making terrific snap judgments; and you can also be intelligent and reflective, making good judgments after thinking things through very carefully.

We are a highly social species. Never, in our evolutionary history as humans, did we survive on our own, as separate individuals. We always depended on our cooperative relationships with others and the same is true today. From this point of view, it is not surprising that natural selection would have supported a broad range of personality types. People of different personalities are well adapted to make different kinds of contributions to the community (and, thereby, also to themselves). Ideally, they would all be valued for the unique contributions they can make and would be helped by others in their areas of weakness. Certainly this was true in hunter-gatherer bands, and we see it operating today within healthy families, tight-knit friendship groups, and well-run businesses. The dimension of control versus impulsivity is, I suggest, one of the most obvious and important dimensions of normal, healthy personality variation. In the course of our evolution, it was valuable that some of us were relatively more controlled and reflective while others of us were relatively less controlled and more action-oriented than the majority.

It is not hard at all to think of conditions in which ADHD-like characteristics are socially valuable (see, for example, Jensen et al., 1997). Distractibility may result in efficient monitoring of changes in the environment, so that sudden dangers or new opportunities, which others would have missed, are detected. Impatience may be a valuable counterweight to the tendency to dwell too long on a way of thinking or behaving that isn't going anywhere. Impulsive action may underlie bravery in the face of dangers that would keep others immobile. Difficulty following instructions may imply independence of mind, which can lead to novel ways of seeing and doing things. Emotional reactivity may be a good counterweight to the tendency of overly controlled people to hold in their emotions and ruminate. One thing I have observed (informally) in people diagnosed with ADHD is that they rarely hold grudges; they let their emotions out and then get over it.

But in school, of course, all of these things are bad; they all get you into trouble. School—at least school as usually defined these days—is a place where you must concentrate on what you are told to concentrate on, no matter how tedious; follow the teachers' directions, no matter how inane; complete assignments for the sheer purpose of completing them, even though they accomplish nothing useful; and, while doing all of that, control your emotions. The school classroom is not a place that values bravery, inventiveness, independence of mind, or emotional reactivity. So, of course, impulsiveness comes across as a "disorder" in school. Today we tend to define school as the primary environment of the child, so impulsiveness is the number one mental disorder of childhood.

Brain Mechanism Underlying the Controlled-Impulsive Dimension of Personality

Neuroscientists have made much-touted progress in understanding the brain, but still that understanding is extremely superficial. We have no idea, really, how the brain does any of the amazing things it does (beyond the simplest reflexes), but we do have some ideas about which parts of the brain are most involved in which functions. The areas of the brain most crucial for executive control appear to lie within the prefrontal lobes of the cerebral cortex and in connections between the prefrontal cortex and other parts of the brain (including the striatum and the basal ganglia), which are involved in initiating and inhibiting actions. At least some of these neural connections involve dopamine as the predominant neurotransmitter, which is significant because the stimulant drugs used most often to treat ADHD—preparations of amphetamine or methylphenidate—all exert their effects by prolonging the action of dopamine in neural synapses.

Not surprisingly, therefore, researchers looking for brain correlates of ADHD have focused on the prefrontal cortex and dopamine. The results of such research are highly variable from lab to lab, with much controversy resulting. Also, the results are often confounded because most of the people in the ADHD groups have been treated with stimulant drugs, either at the time of study or in the past, so it is not clear if any brain difference observed is a correlate of the ADHD itself or is caused by long-term effects of the drug. However, overall, the research suggests that people with ADHD, compared to other people, may have (a) slightly reduced neural mass in the prefrontal cortex, (b) reduced activity in some parts of the prefrontal cortex while performing certain tests of executive function; and (c) fewer dopamine receptors in certain parts of the brain that receive input from the prefrontal cortex. All of these differences are highly variable from individual to individual and observable only as a result of statistical averaging. So far no biological marker of ADHD has been found that is sufficiently reliable to be used as an aid in diagnosis (Mayes & colleagues, 2009).

The studies of brain differences are interesting, but they have no bearing at all on the question of whether ADHD is a disorder or a normal personality variation. All personality variations have a basis in the brain. Of course they do. The brain controls all of behavior, so any difference that is reflected in behavior must exist in the brain. The only means by which natural selection can produce personality variation is through altering genes that affect the brain. If people diagnosed with ADHD differ behaviorally in any consistent way from other people, then their brains must in some way be different. Even if the research to date showed no difference at all in the brains of people with and without an ADHD diagnosis, I would argue that a difference exists. The researchers just haven't looked in the right places, or with the right tools or systems of measurement.

Potential Risks of the Stimulant Drugs
Used in ADHD Treatment

The stimulants used to treat ADHD are powerful drugs that alter radically the chemical environment of the brain, and we don't know their long-term effects in humans. Their immediate side effects are well documented. In degrees that vary from drug to drug and person to person, the drugs can cause insomnia, anorexia, weight loss, suppression of growth in young children, headaches, Tourette's Syndrome, dullness of mind, depression, psychotic episodes, and a host of other negative effects that the drug companies are required to list. Some people cannot tolerate the drugs at all because of these effects, but most, through experimentation, can find a stimulant drug and a dose that is tolerable.

The drugs do, in most people, improve school performance. Students complete more assignments and get higher grades when taking the drugs than when they don't. This is true even for students who are not unusually impulsive and have never been diagnosed with ADHD. That is why many non-ADHD students in high school and college take the drugs illicitly. They commonly get them from ADHD-diagnosed students who secretly aren't taking the drugs. There is no evidence that the drugs improve long-term learning and retention of information, but they definitely improve school performance and grades in the short run (Mayes et al, 2009).

The use of stimulants to improve school performance is somewhat analogous to the use of steroids to improve athletic performance. In both cases the highly competitive environment promotes use of the drugs. Teachers, parents, and students themselves see that the drugs improve performance on standardized tests, and all regard that as a good thing. In our school-obsessed society, performance on such tests has become, more or less, the measure of a person's worth, so anything that improves such performance is worth the discomfort it may produce. Now, as preschools are becoming more and more like elementary schools, with assignments and tests, we are seeing a rapid rise in the number of preschool children—in the age range of 2 to 4—being given the drugs (Mayes et al, 2009). Nobody knows what long-term effects the drugs may be having on those little children's developing brains.

In fact, nobody knows the long-term effects of the drugs on anyone's brain. One possibility, which has some research support, is that the drugs prevent the normal developmental processes that lead most people to become less impulsive, more controlled, as they grow beyond childhood and adolescence. Today we see more and more people who retain the diagnosis of ADHD into adulthood and continue to take stimulant drugs. Is that partly because many of those adults were taking stimulants during earlier stages of their development, which may have interfered with normal brain development? Studies with animals have shown quite clearly that the drugs can have such effect, but so far studies testing this hypothesis in people have not been conducted.

In general, psychoactive drugs do have long-term effects, and most often those effects are in the direction of increasing long-term dependence on the drugs. An interesting and still controversial example concerns the use of antipsychotic drugs to treat schizophrenia. These have long been considered to be the wonder drugs of modern psychiatry, as they make patients with schizophrenia more manageable and often allow them to live independently outside of mental hospitals. On the other hand, we now know that in developing countries, where drug treatment for schizophrenia is much less common than it is in developed countries, people are much more likely to overcome the disorder as they grow older (Hopper et al, 2007). One quite reasonable interpretation of this observation is that the drug treatments turn what would be a temporary condition into a chronic condition (see Gray, 2010b, pp 643-644).

Might the same be true for ADHD? At this point we don't know. Drug companies have no incentive to conduct or support such studies—neither for schizophrenia nor for ADHD—and the studies required to answer the question would take too long and are too complex to make good doctoral dissertations. Even with the best of will, such studies are almost impossible to conduct in a way that produces clearly interpretable results. For ethical and legal reasons, you can't randomly assign people to different treatment conditions and follow them over a prolonged period, as would be required for a true experiment.

You can, however, conduct such experiments with animals, and the animal research to date suggests that the stimulant drugs indeed may produce long-term effects in the direction of prolonging the ADHD condition. In one study, George Ricaurte and his colleagues (2005) assigned one group of monkeys to treatment with Adderall (one of the most common drugs for ADHD) and assigned the other group to placebo treatment. They gave the Adderall orally, at a dose that produced the same blood level of drug that would normally be found in human beings treated for ADHD. After four weeks on Adderall they stopped the treatment for two weeks, then killed the animals and examined their brains. The main result was that the ADHD-treated monkeys showed a 30% to 50% reduction in dopamine and in dopamine transporter molecules in the striatum, which is one of the brain areas considered to be crucial for impulse control. At this point nobody knows what would happen with drug treatments longer than four weeks, and nobody knows if a longer period of recovery following termination of the drug would or would not result in a renewal of normal levels of striatal dopamine.

Given the unknowns and the suggested dangers that come from the animal research, I think we should err on the side of caution in treating ADHD with stimulant drugs. Our first line of attack should be to find alternative means of schooling, so that people can learn in their own chosen ways and are not judged by performance on standardized tests. Then, drug treatment should be reserved only for those few individuals who are so impulsive that they cannot function well or live happily in any of the niches available in our society.

References

Barkley, R., et al. (1997). Behavioral inhibition, sustained attention, and executive functions: Constructing a unified theory of ADHD," *Psychological Bulletin*, 121, 65-95.

Gray, P. (2010a). Assessing normalcy in an abnormal environment. Freedom to Learn blog, *Psychology Today*. Downloaded at https://www.psychologytoday.com/us/blog/freedom-learn/201007/
adhd-school-assessing-normalcy-in-abnormal-environment

Gray (2010b), *Psychology*, 6th edition. New York: Worth.

Hopper, K., et al. (2007). *Recovery from schizophrenia: An international perspective*. Oxford, UK: Oxford University Press.

Jensen, P., et al., Evolution and revolution in child psychiatry: ADHD as a disorder of adaptation. *Journal of the American Academy of Child and Adolescent Psychiatry*, 36, 1672-1681.

Mayes, R., et al. (2009). *Medicating children: ADHD and pediatric mental health*. Cambridge, MA: Harvard University Press.

Ricaurte, G., et al. (2005). Amphetamine treatment similar to that used in the treatment of ADHD damages dopamine nerve endings in the striatum of adult nonhuman primates. *Journal of Pharmacology and Experimental Therapeutics*, 315, 91-98.

16

ADHD, Creativity, and the Concept of Group Intelligence

Two brains that work differently are better than two that work in the same way.

MARCH 25, 2016

I happened across a research article the other day that reported a surprising, counterintuitive finding that got me thinking about a number of things—ADHD, its possible relationship to creativity, and the evolution of intelligence. Let me explain.

In an experiment, inclusion of a person with ADHD greatly improved the problem-solving ability of groups, even though it led to more off-task behavior.

The article was by Sydney Zentall and colleagues (2011), at Purdue University. They were interested in the social behaviors of children with symptoms of ADHD and how those behaviors might affect the actions of those with whom they were interacting. To conduct the experiment, they formed groups consisting of three middle-school students per group. The experimental groups contained one student with ADHD symptoms and two without such symptoms, and the control groups contained only students without the symptoms. In order to give the groups something to interact about, they presented each with two problems to solve—the same two problems for each group. The problems were such that solving them required both insight and logic. The researchers' primary interest was in the cooperative and apparently uncooperative ways the individuals in each group interacted with one another as they attempted to solve the problems.

Here's what they found concerning social interactions. As predicted, the ADHD students often made irrelevant and uncooperative comments, which diverted the group's attention away from the problem to be solved. This kind of behavior was contagious; the non-ADHD students in the experimental groups also showed less cooperative and more off-task behavior than did the non-ADHD students in the control groups. So far this all points against the value of including someone with ADHD in your group.

But now, here's the surprising finding. The groups containing an ADHD student were far more likely to solve the problems than were the control groups! In fact, 14 of the 16 groups (88%) containing an ADHD student solved both problems, and none (0%) of the 6 control groups did. This result was significant at the p < .0001 level, meaning that there is less than one chance in 10,000 that such a large difference, with this many groups, would occur by chance.

What is going on here? How is it that the groups that were

least cooperative and apparently most off-task were able to solve the problems so much more reliably than the highly cooperative groups without an ADHD-disrupter?

The authors of the article give us no clue, at least not in this article. Their main purpose was to score the degree of cooperation and disruption going on, and those results fit their prediction—the ADHD-contaminated groups behaved in ways that appeared less cooperative and less task-oriented than the non-contaminated groups. The researchers weren't particularly interested, in this study, in whether or not the groups actually solved the problems. They reported the problem-solving results as unpredicted and surprising but did not discuss them at all. Their methodology included no observations concerning the actual contributions that each group participant played toward solving the problem. Were the ADHD kids solving the problems themselves? Or were they contributing some unique insight that then helped the others solve the problems? Or were the ADHD kids, perhaps by way of their "disruptive behavior, loosening the thinking of the whole group, which improved everyone's problem-solving ability?

I should note that the "ADHD students" in this experiment were not students who had officially been diagnosed with ADHD. Rather, they were students who were scored by their teachers as having the characteristics of ADHD, using the official diagnostic checklist, but had never been labeled so by a physician. An advantage of this over using officially diagnosed ADHD students is that none of them were taking the stimulant drugs typically used as treatment. So these were non-drugged students with ADHD-like characteristics.

The results led me to wonder if there is other research indicating that peoples with ADHD symptoms are better than others at solving certain kinds of problems. So, I did a little digging into the research literature, and here is what I found.

ADHD symptoms improve "out-of-the-box" thinking and interfere with "in-the-box" thinking.

It turns out that quite a few research studies have been conducted to compare ADHD participants with non-ADHD participants in problem-solving ability. Indeed, Zentall has been involved in some of that work. In one study, he and colleagues found that teenagers who had been identified as "gifted" and who also showed symptoms of ADHD scored higher on the Torrence Tests of Creative Thinking (a standard test of creativity) than did similarly gifted, non-ADHD teenagers (Fugate, Zentall, & Gentry, 2013).

Another study found that 40% of ten-to-twelve-year-olds who had been previously identified as highly creative displayed ADHD symptoms at levels sufficiently high as to warrant diagnosis of the "disorder" (Healy & Rucklidge, 2006). Another study found that ADHD children told more richly imaginative stories than did non-ADHD children (Zentall, 1988). Another found that ADHD teenagers were better at coming up with novel ideas for new toys and were less constrained by examples of old toys than were non-ADHD teenagers (Abraham et al., 2006). Another found that ADHD college students outperformed non-ADHD students in the Unusual Uses Task (where you think of unusual uses for objects (White & Shah, 2006). Another study found that ADHD college students preferred problems that involve generating new ideas, while non-ADHD students preferred problems that involve elaborating upon or extending old ideas (White & Shag, 2011). Yet another found that children who had been diagnosed with ADHD performed better on a test of creative elaboration when they were off of Ritalin (the drug used to treat the "disorder") than when they were on Ritalin (Swartwood et al., 2003).

Taking all of the research together, the studies indicate that ADHD symptoms correspond with improved performance on tasks that involve divergent, or "out-of-the-box" thinking, but interfere with tasks that involve convergent, or "in-the-box" thinking. ADHD students generally perform poorly in school, because school involves almost entirely in-the-box thinking. In fact, thinking out of the box can get you in trouble in school.

So, here's my hypothesis about what was going on in those groups of middle-school children that contained someone with ADHD symptoms: The ADHD kid was generating new ideas about how to solve the problem, and the non-ADHD kids were following through on those ideas in a more focused way to see which ones would actually work. So, even though a lot of tomfoolery was going on in those groups, efficient problem-solving still occurred. In contrast, the groups with no ADHD kid may have been stuck in the mud because nobody was coming up with new ways of trying to solve the problem. They kept persisting—in a highly cooperative, focused, and teacher-pleasing way—on a route that seemed most obvious but wasn't working. I wonder if this hypothesis could be tested in a new analysis of the videotapes from that study.

The Concept of Group Intelligence, and a Theory About the Evolution of Intelligence

Now I move on to a much larger point, about the nature of intelligence and its evolution. We think of intelligence as belonging to an individual person. We measure it in individuals and give it a number, assigned to that individual. Intelligence tests were first developed as a means of predicting school performance, and in schools, as we generally know them, problem-solving is almost always done by individuals, not by groups.

I suggest here that, from an evolutionary perspective, it makes more sense to think of intelligence as a product of the group rather than a product of the individual. During all but a tiny recent portion of our evolutionary history, we were all hunter-gatherers; and research on hunter-gatherers indicates that essentially all of their problem-solving was done by groups (see, for example, Gray, 2009). Men tracked and hunted in groups, and to do so they had to solve many very difficult intellectual problems. Indeed, a whole book has been written on the theme that the mental skills involved in tracking mark the origin of science (Liebenberg, 1990). As pointed out by one anthropologist (Wannenburgh,1979), the men involved in tracking would discuss and test various hypotheses about the meaning of the scant signs in the sand, or the way a particular branch was bent, in order to determine such issues as the species, size, speed of movement of the animal and the time of day that it had passed that spot. Similarly, women generally worked in groups to decide where and what to gather on a given day, based on cues as to what might be available in the area where they were foraging. In the evening, around the campfire, all of them would be involved in making decisions that affected the whole band, such as whether or not it was time to move on to a new camp site and where that camp site might be.

It's easy to understand why problem solving in these situations would be facilitated by including people with diverse cognitive styles. In particular, in relation to the ADHD research, it would seem valuable to have one or more persons in your group whose attention is easily distracted and who, therefore, shifts quickly from one observation or idea to another. In the hunting group, that's the person who would notice a bit of fur stuck to a thorn, which the others had missed because they were so busy focusing on and debating about the mark in the sand. That's also the person who might hear a tiger in the distance, and warn the others, who had missed that because it was irrelevant to the immediate problem they were trying to solve. Sometimes the ADHD guy might save the lives of the more studious, stuck-in-the-mud non-ADHD individuals.

I am suggesting that, historically, intelligence was the product of a network of minds working together, sometimes at odds with one another. And, in many if not most cases outside of school, that is still true today.

I have a long-time friend who is famous for his ability to put together great scientific teams. He currently heads a science department at one of the world's most prestigious universities. I once asked him for his opinion about what makes a good scientist. I don't remember his exact words, but the gist was something like this: Science is really a group enterprise. One person might get the Nobel Prize for something, but that person always benefitted from the work and ideas of others. You need some people who are basically good stamp collectors. They just like to collect and organize things. You need others who like to monkey around with equipment. They are the ones who work out practical ways to do the research you want to do. You need others who are kind of impractical and wild in their thinking. They come up with all sorts of ideas, many of them crazy, but some of them not so crazy, some even brilliant. Then you need people who are good at sorting through ideas to see which ones fit the facts and to follow them up logically with well-designed studies. I suspect that the research teams my friend has built are not devoid of people with symptoms of ADHD.

References

Abraham, A., et al (2006). Creative thinking in adolescents with attention deficit hyperactivity disorder (ADHD). *Child Neuropsychology*, 12, 111-123.

Forster, S., & Lavie, N. (2016) Establishing the attention-distractibility trait. *Psychological Science*, 27, 203-212.

Fugate, C. M., Zentall, S. S., & Gentry, M. (2013). Creativity and working memory in gifted students with and without characteristics of Attention Deficit Hyperactivity Disorder: Lifting the mask. *Gifted Child Quarterly*, 57, 234-246.

Gray, P. (2009). Play as a foundation for hunter-gatherer social existence. *American Journal of Play*, 1, 476-522.

Healy, D., & Rucklidge, J. (2006) An investigation into the relationship among ADHD symptomatology, creativity, and neuropsychological functioning in children. *Child Neuropsychology*, 12, 421-438.

Liebenberg, L. (1990). *The art of tracking: The origin of science*. Capetown: David Philip Publishers.

Swartwood, M., Swartwood, J., & Farrell, J. (2003). Stimulant treatment of ADHD: Effects on creativity and flexibility of problem solving. *Creativity Research Journal*, 15, 417-419.

Wannenburgh, A. (1979). *The Bushmen*. Secaucus, NJ: Chartwell Publishers.

White, H., & Shah, P. (2006). Uninhibited imaginations: Creativity in adults with Attention-Deficit/Hyperactivity Disorder. *Personality and Individual Differences*, 40, 1121-1131.

White, H., & Shah, P. (2011). Creative style and achievement in adults with attention-deficit/hyperactivity disorder. *Personality and Individual Differences*, 50, 673-677.

Zentall, S. S. (1988). Production deficiencies in elicited language but not in the spontaneous verbalizations of hyperactive children. *Journal of Abnormal Child Psychology*, 16, 657-673.

Zentall, S., Kuester, D., & Craig, B. (2011). Social behavior in cooperative groups: Students at risk for ADHD and their peers. *Journal of Educational Research*, 104, 28-41.

17

The Value of Mind Wandering in Solving Difficult Problems

*Some problems can be solved best by
taking a break from trying to solve them.*

FEBRUARY 7, 2019

I begin by listing four quite striking, possibly counterintuitive findings from research on problem solving.

1. People who show the symptoms of ADHD—notably, a tendency to be easily distracted from the task at hand—have been repeatedly found to be much better at solving certain kinds of problems than are people who don't show these symptoms. I summarized and referenced some of the evidence for this in the essay just preceding this one in the collection (also see Boot, Nevicka, & Baas (2017).

2. People who, because of strokes or tumors, have suffered damage to the prefrontal lobes of the cortex (brain areas that help focus attention and help develop conscious

problem-solving strategies) have been found to be much better than people with intact brains at solving certain kinds of problems (Reverberi et al., 2005).

3. Brain-intact people have been found to show great improvement at solving certain kinds of problems if a portion of their prefrontal lobes has been temporarily rendered less active by a process called transcranial direct current stimulation, which involves a slight electric current sent across the skull over a particular brain area (Luft et al, 2017).

4. Dozens of experiments have shown that people who are stumped in solving certain kinds problem are subsequently much more likely to solve the problem if they take a break, in which they think about something else for awhile, than they are if they work continuously on the problem (for reviews, see Sio et al, 2017; Sio & Ormerod, 2009). This is called the "incubation effect." A number of studies have shown that the incubation effect works best when, during incubation, the person is just daydreaming or working on some relatively easy set of tasks rather than focusing heavily on a new problem.

What are these "certain kinds of problems"? They are problems that cannot be solved through one's routine, ingrained, well-trained ways of thinking. They are sometimes called "insight problems," because, when you finally do solve them, the solution seems to jump out from nowhere, and you experience the classic "aha" phenomenon. Suddenly you see what you didn't see before. It seems magical. From where did that solution come?

The solution must have come somehow from the unconscious mind. Our brain is an amazing machine that is always working on many things at once. Our conscious experience of thought, which generally runs along a single track rather than many at once, reflects only a small portion of what the brain is doing. On this, if on nothing else, Freud was right: The conscious mind is just the tip of the iceberg. Apparently, when we stop thinking consciously about the problem that we have been unable to solve, the unconscious mind takes the problem on and continues to work on it in some way— not through the logical means of the conscious mind, but through some other kind of logic. There are various theories about what the unconscious mind is doing. One prominent theory is that it is checking out a broad range of potential links between elements of the problem and other information stored in memory, including links that are too remote for the conscious, logical mind to consider. Suddenly, the mind hits a link that works, that solves the problem, and this awakens the conscious mind—"Aha, I see it now!"

On the basis of this theory, people with ADHD, or with damage to the prefrontal lobe, or with a temporarily suppressed prefrontal lobe, are more likely to solve such problems than are other people because they are less able to maintain fixed attention. They are more likely to allow their mind to wander and, therefore, more likely to allow the unconscious mechanisms to take over.

All the research I've referenced so far was done in laboratories, with insight problems created specifically for research purposes. What about real-world problem solving? In a recent study, Shelly Gable, Elizabeth Hopper, and Jonathan Schooler, of the University of California, Santa Barbara. (2019), recruited 72 theoretical physicists and 113 professional writers (mostly screenwriters) as participants in a study of problem solving related to their professions. Each participant was emailed a questionnaire each evening, for two weeks, which asked them to describe the most creative idea, if any, they had that day related to their work. If they listed an idea, they were asked questions about what they were doing and thinking when they had the idea, and whether it entailed overcoming an impasse or felt like an "aha" moment, and how important and creative the idea was.

Of most interest for our purposes, the researchers found that approximately 20% of the creative ideas, for both physicists and writers, occurred at times when they were not thinking about the problem to which the idea pertained. They occurred while they were away from their work and thinking about something else. Moreover, these ideas were especially likely to be experienced as "aha" moments and to contain solutions to problems for which they had previously been at an impasse—that is, at a point where the problem had begun to seem unsolvable.

Decades ago, long before I had ever heard of research like what I've described here, I discovered that the best thing for me to do when I am stuck on some problem—be it a problem of research design, or writing, or even a personal relationship problem—is to take a break. For me, the best kind of break is to go outside for a walk or a bike ride, or to work in my garden or chop wood for my stove, and just let my mind go free as I do so. Not always, but quite often I find that some insightful idea that solves or helps to solve the problem comes to mind as I'm traipsing through the woods or peddling down the road or mulching the tomatoes or splitting logs. And even when no idea pops up, I haven't wasted time. My breaks produce good exercise, fun, tomatoes, and firewood.

Sometimes when no solution comes during the break, one comes very quickly after I come back to the problem. I figure in those cases that my unconscious mind had come pretty close to the solution and it just took a little further conscious attention to bring it forth. Nowadays I go outdoors for at least an hour's adventure of some sort nearly every day, whether or not I feel stuck on a problem. Often new creative ideas pop into my mind that have nothing to do with problems I've been working on, but that suggest new projects that would be well worth taking on.

Usually in my essays I urge you to let your children run free. So now, in concluding this one, I note that among the many good things that happen when anyone runs free—whether it is you or your child or anyone else—is that the person's mind runs free. The mind, in that freedom, may be working on things that have nothing to do with what the body is doing.

References

Boot, N., Nevicka, B., & Baas, M. (2017). Subclinical symptoms of attention-deficit/hyperactivity disorder (ADHD) are associated with specific creative processes. *Personality and Individual Difference*, 114, 73-81.

Gable, S. L., Hopper, E. A., & Schooler, J. W. (2019). When the muses strike: Creative ideas of physicists and writers routinely occur during mind wandering. *Psychological Science*, 30, 396-404.

Luft, C. D. B., Zioga, I., Banissy, M. J., & Bhattacharya, J. (2017). Relaxing learning constraints through cathodal tDCS on the dorsolateral prefrontal corex. *Scientific Reports*, 7, 2916.

Reverberi, C., Toraldo, A., D'Agostini, S., & Skrap, M. (2005). Better without (lateral) frontal cortex? Insight problems solved by frontal patients. *Brain*, 128, 2882-2890.

Sio, U. N., & Ormerod, T. C. (2009). Does incubation enhance problem solving? A meta-analytic review. *Psychological Bulletin*, 135, 94-120.

Sio, U. N., Kotovsky, K., & Cagan, J. (2017). Interrupted: The role of distributed effort and incubation in preventing fixation and generating problem solutions. *Memory and Cognition*, 45, 553-565.